Belgium Tour Guide

Tourism

Author
Jesse Russell.

First Printed: 2019.

Publisher:
SONITTEC LTD
College House, 2nd
Floor
17 King Edwards
Road,
Ruislip
London
HA4 7AE .

Table of Content

Summary

How Traveling Can Broaden Your Perspective

Belgium Tour Guide: You may not need a lot of convincing when it comes to finding a reason to travel especially when considering a trip to a foreign country. Exploring the world, seeing new places, and learning about new cultures are just a few of the benefits of traveling. There is value to exploring someplace new and combating the stress of getting out of your comfort zone.

Traveling should be looked at as a journey for personal growth, mental health, and spiritual enlightenment. Taking the time to travel to a new place can both literally and figuratively open your eyes to things you have never seen before. These new experiences allow you to get to know yourself in ways you can't if you stay in the same place.

Traveling is wonderful in so many ways:

- ✓ You can indulge your sense of wanderlust.
- ✓ You experience different cultures.

✓ Your taste buds get to experience unique foods.

✓ You meet all different kinds of people.

As you grow older, your mind evolves and expands to adapt to the new information you receive. Traveling to a new destination is similar in this way, but the learning process occurs at a faster rate. Traveling thrusts you into the unknown and delivers you with a bounty of new information and ideas. The expansion of your mind is one of the greatest benefits of travel. Keep reading to learn six more benefits of traveling.

>Discover Your Purpose: Feeling as though you have a purpose in life is more important than many people realize. A purpose connects you to something bigger than yourself and keeps you moving forward. Your purpose in life can change suddenly and fluidly as you enter new stages in becoming who you are. With each new stage in life, there comes new goals and callings. Traveling can help open your eyes to a new life direction. You may be wandering down a path unaware of where you will end up. Seeing new places and meeting new people can help you break from that path and discover what your true purpose is.

Traveling is an excellent remedy for when you feel you need to refocus on your purpose and goals, or re-evaluate your life path. There is no better time to open your eyes than when your life seems to be out of focus and in need of redirection. You might just be surprised by what you discover and find a new sense of life purpose how traveling changes you.

Traveling is a way to discover parts of yourself that you never knew existed. While traveling, you have no choice but to deal with unexpected situations. For example, how you may typically handle a problem at home might be a completely unacceptable approach when you are in an unfamiliar place without all of the comforts and conveniences of home.

>Be Aware of Your Blessings: When you travel to a new destination, your eyes are opened to new standards, and, you become more aware of all the blessings and privileges you have been given. It is easy to forget what you do have and only focus on what is missing from your life. Traveling can help put things back into perspective and re-center your priorities on what truly matters.

Consider traveling through an area that has no electricity or running water if you come from a place where cold bottled water is easily accessible and nearly anything you want can be delivered to your door in less than an hour. These are two completely different worlds and ways of living. For people who experience a more privileged quality of life, seeing others who live in drastically different situations can help you appreciate what you have and spark an interest for you to lend support to people living elsewhere.

>Find Truth: There's concept, and then there's experience. You can know things from reading them online and listening to a lecture, but to experience something in person is different.

Traveling can help open your eyes to the true kindness and goodness of humanity. There is a myth that when you travel you are on your own, but that simply is not the case. The welcoming attitude and overwhelming hospitality that people give to travelers may be one of the most surprising truths about traveling. Beyond that, you have the whole world to learn about with every place you discover, through every person you meet and every culture you experience.

>Expand Your Mind: A key benefit of traveling, or taking the opportunity to explore on a vacation, is being given the opportunity to expand your mind in ways you can't imagine. If you can allow yourself to travel with an open mind and accept the new experiences and adventures around you, you give your mind the chance to see the world from a new perspective.

Think of it as a spiritual and intellectual enlightenment. You never stop being curious and should always seek out education whenever possible throughout your life. You are doing a disservice to yourself if you choose to close yourself off from the world. It is not always easy to let new ideas in, especially when they are in direct contrast with what you may believe. You have everything you need to grow, you just have to allow yourself to do it.

>Connect to Others: It's easy to forget how similar you are to others, regardless of where you come from, what your background is, or how much money you have. At the end of the day, human beings share more in common with one another than they may choose to admit. When taking a trip to a different country, you may have learned to cast aside what is different and unusual because from the outside, others may not look or act alike. But if you give yourself a chance, you may be surprised to find how minimal and superficial these differences are.

As you notice how you share similar needs, your perspective of your home expands, you become friends with people from different backgrounds and cultures, you realize how everyone is connected. This state of awareness is a jump in consciousness that can help you experience a world-centric view of consciousness—more expansive and aware.

>Break Out of Your Shell: Without a doubt, one of the benefits of traveling is that it forces you to step out of your bubble, which can provide you with many emotional health benefits. Yes, it may be uncomfortable and scary to break away from your daily routine, but the rewards are worth it. What you gain in experience and knowledge may outweigh any amount of doubt or apprehension you had before embarking on your journey. Travel also helps you to self-reflect and dig deep into who you are as a person.

Something magical happens when people are put in new situations than they are normally faced with in their everyday life, as behavior becomes more raw and real as a result of being out of your conditioned environment. This not-so-subtle push into the world helps you to become more open and comfortable expressing yourself without the worry of feeling judged.

>See the Big Picture: Life is a limited gift. You must choose to make the most of each day. As you travel and experience more of the world, you may be struck with gratitude and appreciation for all the places you have enjoyed and people you've shared your travels with. You have the power to take control of your life and can inspire you to start doing more..

About Belgium
Belgium Introduction

According to legend, the two most notable things about Belgium are that it's flat, and its natives only eat chips if they're smothered in gallons of mayonnaise. Both, of course, are absolutely true, at least in part, but there's a greater deal more to see, do, and enjoy in this small country than the landscape and snack food.

Belgium is split into three regions; the Walloon and Flemish sectors and the Brussels-Capital Region. Belgians in the southern Walloon region speak French and/or German dependent on the location, the Flemish community speaks Dutch, the small capital region is decidedly multi-lingual, with English spoken to some extent across the country. The three communities differ markedly in regards to culture, but all welcome visitors.

History buffs will be in heaven, with traces of powerful dynasties that held the country during the medieval period still visible everywhere, especially in the town of Bruges, where Belgium's 14th century

'Golden Age' is visibly remnant. The vibrant capital city of Brussels isn't just a hub for European politicians; it's also a center for culture, theater, great dining, nightlife and shopping, and holds guilded houses, Gothic buildings, a castle, the Royal Palace, as well as post-modern structures. Ghent is another place to head if magnificent architectural treasures appeal to you.

The 'Belgium is flat' brigade may be surprised to learn that forests, caves, and cliffs of the Ardennes lie within the country's borders. This spectacular region is home to deer, wild boar, and lynx, as well as charming little villages, ancient castles, and the fine city of Nemur, set along the River Meuse. Nemur is a great base for exploring the beauties of the Ardennes. The national art museums in Brussels and Antwerp display works by famous Belgian masters, and Brussels boasts 80 museums of all kinds, including a number covering both World Wars.

Accommodation across the country varies from luxury five-star hotels to mid-range country inns and self-catered apartments. Standards are high, as are prices in the better Brussels hotels, but are surprisingly reasonable outside the urban centers. Dining out is popular and there's a huge choice of cuisines available at all price points. Belgian cuisine has its regional variations and is filling and delicious, with seafood a favorite and mussels a specialty. Lovers of chocolate know full well that the Belgian version reign supreme, with impossible-toresist chocolate shops on nearly every corner. It is also one of the best cities for beer.

The small size of Belgium and its position in the heart of Europe makes exploration of the country on day trips a comfortable experience, and allows for trips to Northern France, Luxembourg, the Netherlands, and Germany, dependent on your base location as a bonus. To the south are the battlegrounds and cemeteries from two World Wars, and the diamond district of Antwerp is close to Brussels, as is the lovely Sonian Forest. The golfing scene is extensive, with the best courses an easy drive of the capital.

Public transport in Belgium is fast, efficient, and inexpensive when compared to neighboring Germany and the UK. The main cities of Brussels, Namur, and Antwerp are linked by train and, for shorter journeys, buses are the best choice. For those planning to make several stops, a rail pass can save money. Brussels has trams and a subway, and for getting around just about every city and town, cycling is a healthy alternative to taxis, with bike rental shops plentiful and available.

Belgium Sightseeing

Travel guide attractions, sights, nature and touristic places
You will find many interesting places in Belgium. Nearly every town of the country is home to beautiful castles, churches and cathedrals,

3

medieval buildings and museums. The best way to start your acquaintance with Belgium is to visit Brussels.

The old part of the city is the most interesting place for tourists. Locals call old town in a very unusual way Pentagon. The district was called this way because of numerous circle shaped boulevards that were built instead of former protective facilities. Grand Place Square is a must visit place for all tourists. The building of City Hall is also located on the square. The Museum of Brussels is located on the opposite side, and the historic district of the city starts right after the square. That place is a must visit one for tourists, as the majority of centuries old buildings, churches and squares are located there. The Royal Galleries of Saint-Hubert are one of the most famous landmarks of Brussels. This is an architectural complex that combines theatres, art galleries and museums. There are several dozen of public places there.

Continue your travel in Belgium by visiting the city of Anderlecht. The most important sights of the city include the Museum of Erasmus of Rotterdam, Astrid Park, Gaasbeek Castle and Constant Vanden Stock Stadium. The city of Antwerpen is famous for its numerous museums. There are more than 30 museums in total in the city. The most famous ones are the Royal Museum of Art, Plantin Moretus Museum, Mayer Van Den Bergh Museum, the Museum of Modern Art, the Museum of National Art and Ethnography, the Museum of Sculptures and Folklore Museum. There are also architectural places of interest in Belgium, the most famous ones being Bodenbond Tower and Royal Palace built back the 18th century.

The town of Lier is also worth closest attention. The most famous sights of the town are Zimmer Tower and old astronomy clock. Continue your travel, and you will reach Kalmthout Nature Reserve that is located nearby. The reserve features simply unforgettable combination of sand dunes and dense forests. Tourists, who wish to see more historic places, are welcome to visit Gent, the central part of which is a true open-air museum. Such magnificent sights as St. Bavo's Cathedral, St. Peter's Abbey, Van Der Meer Palace, St. Jacob Church and Royal Palace on Breydelstraat Street are definitely worth closest attention. Travellers, who enjoy going to museums, will be pleased as well as there are more than ten large museums in Gent.

History and Entertainment

Belgium is one of those countries that are considered as universal tourist areas. It will be very interesting for adherents of different entertainments to vacation here. The country is notable for its luxurious beaches, unique attractions and picturesque natural sites. The most famous beach resort is Ostende. The length of its sandy beach is 9 km.

The resort is quite crowded and noisy. Fans of peaceful recreation often prefer the neighboring town of De Panne. Fans of elite recreation usually visit the resort of Knokke-Heist. There are a lot of luxurious hotels and restaurants. Newport is very popular with surfers and yachtsmen. The resort is characterized by a well-developed sports infrastructure.

Belgium is one of the most interesting European countries for spending the Christmas holidays. The city is transformed already in early December. They are decorated with festive lights. There are Christmas markets and fairs everywhere. In summer, on 21 July, the important National Day of Belgium is celebrated.

For many years, Belgian cities have been a place where major international festivals are held. In summer, the jazz festival called Middelheim is organized in Antwerpen. Ostende is notable for its themed fests dedicated to antiques and photography. In June, Audenarde is always visited by connoisseurs of an amber drink. The Beer Festival is annually held here. The greatest festival is the Ghent holidays celebrated in July. For 10 days, Ghent is transformed into a big outdoor concert stage. There are theatrical, musical and dance performances in the city streets and squares.

Belgium has its incomparable food symbols, the most famous of which are waffles and chocolate. Sweet-teeth have an opportunity to visit special shops in any city or town. One of the most popular treats is chocolate from the historical Mary Chocolatier factory. At one time, this company produced chocolate only for the royal family. The most popular national drink is beer. Over 600 sorts of beer are produced in Belgium.

Major sightseeing

Cultural sights

Cultural sightseeing in Belgium. What to visit museums, temples, castles and palaces

Some people mistakenly believe Belgium is not an interesting country to visit. This unfortunate misconception is utterly untrue. In fact, Belgium as a country contains everything necessary for cultural recreation: historical and art museums will acquaint you with the history and art of Belgium, churches, and temples of various denominations will amaze you with their beauty, grandeur, and antiquity, and besides, there are many interesting historical sites on the Belgian land, some of which are listed on the UNESCO World Heritage List. This list includes, for example, the Catholic Cathedral of Our Lady Antwerp. It was erected in a space of 169 years, and in 1521 it was finally open to the parishioners. In this magnificent Gothic building are works of famous artists.

The collegiate church of St. Gertrude is located in Nivelles. It was built ten centuries ago and was first a nunnery. In the early forties of the last century, the church was damaged by Nazi bombs, and its reconstruction was completed only in the mid-eighties. St. Gertrude

Nivelles, the patroness of travelers and the first prioress of the monastery, after whom the church was named, was buried within the walls of the church. Cathedrale Saints-Michel-et-Güdüle is located in Brussels. This is a masterpiece of Gothic architecture, built in the 10th century. It hosts services, art exhibitions, and other cultural events. This Cathedral was built for almost three hundred years, and its main pride is the baroque altar.

The Basilica of the Holy Blood in Bruges is famous not only for its wonderful stained glass windows but also for the legend that a flask with the blood of Jesus Christ is hidden in this building. Two ancient chapels are connected by a staircase, and the smaller one was built in the 12th century. A wonderful, fabulous town will be found by the guests of Bruges in the city center. Many buildings here have been preserved from the Middle Ages. This incredible place is on the UNESCO World Heritage List, and it is so nice to just walk around and get mentally transferred a couple of centuries back. Quiet and calm, the center looks unusual, surrounded by a modern city.

In Brussels, be sure to visit the Belgian Comic Strip Center. It is located in the center of the capital and offers visitors the opportunity to get acquainted with the works of artists who create short comic strips. The museum will be interesting to children and adults, as it is possible not only to watch the adventures of comic book heroes but also to learn the history of their creation. The Museum is open daily from 10 am to 6 pm. Another interesting place in Brussels is the Musical Instruments Museum, created in the seventies of the 19th century. In its four-storey building, visitors will find modern and ancient musical instruments, learn the history of music of the Middle Ages and the Renaissance, as well as get acquainted with musical instruments from different eras from around the world. The Museum is open every day from 9.30am to 5 pm, with the exception of Saturdays and Sundays when it opens from 10 am to 5 pm, and Mondays when it is closed.

The Groeninge Museum in Bruges is renowned for its rich collection of Belgian art from different eras. Pictures of such giants as Jan van Eyck, the earlier works of Belgian artists, neoclassicism and 20th-century art are only part of the collection. In addition to the permanent exhibits, you can see other works within the framework of temporary exhibitions in the museum. The Museum is open every day except Mondays, from 10 am to 5 pm. The city of Antwerp is proud of the Diamond Museum, where every day there is a public demonstration of the polishing of diamonds. An extensive collection will introduce you to the characteristics of the jewel, their extraction, and processing phases. Also, there is a museum of photography (Fotomuseum) in Antwerp, showing the work of Belgian photographers of different years. The museum encourages young photographers in Belgium by displaying their work on its walls. It is better to visit this place without children, as some works can be quite explicit.

The Municipal Museum of Contemporary Art is located in the city of Ghent. Permanent collection and temporary exhibitions offer guests the opportunity to learn a lot about modern art, which is often provocative and controversial. They also get to see the different methods of expressing thoughts, which are used by artists. Those who prefer the classics should visit the Musée des Beaux-Arts in Tournai, which was opened at the very beginning of the 20th century and contains works by Rubens, Monet, Van Gogh, and other famous artists. The building of the museum with its unusual shape brings to mind a turtle.

If you find yourself in Brussels, you are humbly obliged to visit the Grand Place in the City Center, which is considered one of the most beautiful squares in Europe. The square has been in existence since the 13th century. Cultural events are held here, and finally, it is just a pleasure to walk around the square, admiring the buildings with baroque and gothic architecture. In Ypres, there is the Menin Gate, built as a monument to the Belgians who were killed not far from here during the First World War. The bodies of the warriors, which number about half a million, were never found. For the past 90 years, every evening at eight o'clock, the trumpet here sounds, followed by a minute of silence in memory of the dead.

Festivals in Belgium

Fun and festivities in Belgium celebrations, festivals and cultural events

Belgians are unique people. By their number of different holidays and festivals, Belgium firmly holds the lead among European countries. Every year, about 2000 of various festivals, holidays and processions are celebrated and organized here. In Belgium, residents are very careful about their own culture and history. As a result, it is customary in the country to celebrate many festivals with historical roots. That is why Belgian holidays are full of different traditions and customs. But besides this one, as well as the holidays considered official, in Belgium, they also celebrate purely national holidays and dates. Belgian holidays are characterized by mass open festivities, noisy carnivals, processions with songs and dances along the canals.

Christmas night in Belgium is special. When nature fades away, the things which are peculiar signs of the rebirth of life begin to have special meaning. In this regard, it is customary to bring into the house evergreens or representatives of the flora, which come to life in winter. On Christmas, they like to tell legends. In order to scare them away, people fumigate their houses with juniper smoke as well as pass in processions with burning torches or candles all the way around the house.

The Belgians also blow a special horn. On the next day of the holiday, it is customary to attend theaters and concerts and to spend the evening in a restaurant with relatives and friends. A lot of tourists come to Belgium to witness the February carnival in the city of Binche. On the first day, costume marches are held in massive numbers to the city. The next day, round dances are seen in the town square, and fireworks are displayed. The third day is usually the most interesting. Celebrants wearing national clothes and wax masks walk through the city streets and throw oranges at passersby. According to the beliefs of the Belgians, if a person catches this fruit, he will be lucky.

In April, the Belgians hold carnivals in La Louviere and Stavelot. The festival of folklore is also celebrated in this month in Leuven. On the night of April 30th to May 1st, on the eve of celebrating the holiday of spring and labor, the Belgians during the witch dance burn the effigy of winter. On May 13th in the city of Ypres, there is a parade of cats. It was first held in the year 1955 and has been held annually ever since. In the Middle Ages, cats were considered to be a symbol of evil.

The killing of cats was at the time believed to redeem the people from their sins, so the unfortunate cats were thrown down from the central city tower. But today instead of real animals, stuffed animals are flying down in their place. All participants in the action are dressed in costumes and emblems of these cute animals. May 19th starts the celebration of the holiday Doudou. It is celebrated into the whole of the next week. The Belgians celebrate Doudou in honor of the victory over the plague. The tradition of this holiday goes deep into the 14th century, when, after a religious procession in the city of Mons, the disease receded.

Solemn events begin with a procession through the streets of the city, with participants dressed in costumes of the medieval era. Doudou ends with the staged battle of St. George and the dragon. Many centuries ago, the dragon broke into the city streets, but he was defeated by St. George. Since then, each year a procession led by the chariot of the saint makes a circle around Mons, after which the staged battle of the dragon with St. George takes place.

At the beginning of summer, the Belgians celebrate Father's Day, which has become the equivalent of Mother's Day. The main motive of the holiday was the desire to emphasize the role of the father in the family and also in raising the offspring. On June 23rd and 24th, a historical reenactment of the last battle of Emperor Napoleon against the allied army takes place in Waterloo. Participants are dressed in costumes of the early 19th century. Everywhere here you will see a lot of historical props, weapons, and items of a bygone era. During the reenactment, visitors will be able to learn interesting information about weapons, life in bivouacs, watch the preparation of food on fire using old recipes, and shoot at targets.

On July 21st, a military parade is held on the main square of the capital in honor of Independence Day. After its completion, folk festivals begin, where artists of various arts perform. The holiday is brought to an end with large fireworks. In mid-August, the Flower Carpet Festival is held in Brussels. As part of this holiday, volunteers prepare a carpet of fresh flowers on the Grand Place Square. The finished live web extends 75 meters in length and 24 meters in width. Amongst the fragrance of flowers on the square, a musical concert is held.

In mid-October, an international film festival is held in Ghent. Its inaugural history dates back to the year 1974. This festival usually lasts 11 days. The cinema and music interaction has become the primary specialization of the festival. Since 2001, composers who have written soundtracks for films are conferred awards during the festival. November 15th is when the Belgians celebrate the Feast of the Dynasty. Established by the second monarch of Belgium, Leopold II, this day is celebrated in honor of St. Albert, who is considered the heavenly defender of the royal family. The day of the royal dynasty became a symbol of the unity of the Belgians. During this holiday, numerous discussions about the role of the monarchy in the modern life of the country are held throughout the country.

Unique sights

Travel ideas for Belgium unique sights, worth Guinness records

Chateau de Belœil

The Belœil Castle has been one of the most visited castles in Belgium for several years. The first mention of the castle dates back to the 13th century. At the end of the 14th century the castle became the property of the Princes of Ligne and was of great strategic importance until the 17th century. Later, the dark castle under the direction of owner was converted into the chic residence and was used as a venue for balls and official events. The nearby France has influenced the exterior of the building. Today, the building is surrounded by the wonderfully beautiful French garden, whose area is 120 hectares.

In the twentieth century, the castle was transformed into the art museum and presents visitors a unique collection of the old paintings, the age of some of which forms more than 500 years. You can also see the valuable collection of more than 20,000 ancient books in the castle. The adjoining territory is as well as its interior decoration as well worth seeing. During the excursion visitors can see a beautiful pond, as well as a lot of the old stone sculptures and the interesting landscape elements.

The experienced tourists strive to visit the castle at the beginning of corn. For several years it has served as the location of the beautiful flower festival 'Amaryllisfeerie'. In the course of ten days the guests of the castle can enjoy the wonderfully beautiful colors and participate in the exciting cultural events. At the end of August the castle welcomes the followers of classical music. The concerts of the most famous musicians and orchestras take place in the picturesque Schlossgarten.

Water Tower Conversion

In Belgium there are quite unusual houses. One of the most famous among them is the design studio BHAM. The gifted modern designers have converted the old water tower, whose height is 30 meters, into a comfortable house. The diameter of the unusual house is also quite impressive and is 20 meters, and the general area of the six-storey house forms 400 sqm

The water tower, built in 1938 in the town of Stinokkerzil, was expediently used until the end of the 20th century. In the course of this time, the tower became a distinctive architectural landmark, which is why the tower was deserted, the talented architects decided to give the second life to the tower. In 2007 the large tower reconstruction began, which lasted more than three years.

The original construction was completely restored, on the ground floor the garage was furnished. For the convenience of the residents the tower was provided with the elevator. The rooms were designed as minimalism. The modern furnishings of the old tower have nothing in common with the old traditions. The elegant colors and the strict forms weigh in the interior furnishing. The original house in the water tower is environmentally friendly and is designed with the natural materials. In addition, the house uses the alternative energy sources, which makes it even more unique.

Atomium

In Brussels is the unique building Atomium, which can hardly be called a typical building. The structure is a huge model of the iron atom and consists of the large metal spheres connected to the metal tubes. The original building in Brussels was built in 1958 on the occasion of the opening of the World Exhibition, symbolizing scientific progress. Nowadays, Atomium is used as the location of exhibitions and cultural events, most of which are devoted to technical progress.

The height of the construction is 102 meters. In the upper sphere of the gigantic atom, the viewing platform and the cozy restaurant, from which the wonderful panorama of the city opens. One of the spheres is specially designed for children. There are colorful recreation and games rooms. If desired, the parents with the children in one of the rooms can spend the whole day and even stay in it.

The unique building, whose design was developed by the outstanding architect Adre Waterkeyn, is today the landmark of national importance. The huge pipes that connect the spheres have not only a decorative purpose. Inside are the escalators and high-speed trains, with the help of which visitors of the 'atom' can move freely through their entire space. In 2006 the unusual building was completely renovated, after which it even looked more attractive. In the evening Atomium is illuminated by the wonderful illumination. The building is surrounded by the picturesque park with fountains and comfortable recreation areas.

Celebrities Underwear Museum

One of the most extravagant and original museums in the world is in Brussels. Celebrities Underwear Museum presents visitors with literally the most sensual and provocative exhibits. In the museum one can see the underwear of the showbusiness celebrities and the politicians. From some exhibits the museum founder has formed the very original photocollagen. It must be noted that all the garments presented in the museum were not only owned by the celebrities but were attracted at least once.

This important fact is confirmed by the special certificates, which can be seen alongside all the pieces of the original collection. The original collection of the Brussels Museum is not so extensive, it contains only a few dozens of exhibits presented in the only exhibition hall. The founder and owner of the extravagant museum is the Belgian painter Jan Bucquoy. For this reason, the exposition not only covers the small pieces, but also the unique art objects.

All collages presented in the museum are humorous and charming. One of the best collages is, according to the opinion of the museum founder, the collage depicting Nicolas Sarkozy. The talented painter does not want to stand still. He aims to expand the collection of the original museum and to prove to his guests that 'face to face all underwear are the same.

Hallerbos Forest

In Belgium you can also find the strange and little known sights. Such attractions include the fairytale Hallerbos forest. The extensive beech forest, whose surface is 5.5 sq km, is a fairytale because of the wild hyacinths. In the second half of April, these wondrous flowers with the blue bells cover the forest like a lush colorful carpet, forming a beautiful contrast with the young green leaves. The forest looks magical. Most tourists strive to visit it at the end of April or the beginning of May.

Most people who visit the Blue Forest Hallerbos are the locals. This natural sight is not so well known among foreign guests. The travelers, who want to visit the fabulous forest next spring, are to take a trip accompanied by the guide. It does not help to get lost in the unknown forest, and will also show the most interesting places where you can observe the forest inhabitants of the forest from afar.

The forest is located in the surroundings of the town of Dvorp and is only a 30 minute drive from Brussels. The fact that the sight is located in the immediate vicinity of the large industrial centers makes it even more strange. According to the approximate bills, the age of the unique Blue Forest forms about 400 years. The researchers believe that so extensive hyacinth thickening has formed on its territory in the course of a few centuries. Today, the forest is the unique ecosystem that serves as a location for rabbits, deer and rare birds. If you are lucky, you can meet the forest inhabitants during the hike.

Dinner In The Sky

Another great way to enjoy delicious dishes on the heights to book a table at the popular Brussels Dinner Dinner in the Sky. This open-air restaurant is a small platform with transparent canopy which has the height of 50 meters. Once the platform can receive 22 visitors. The guests are served by 4 employees of the restaurant the waiter, the cook, the security man and the musician.

The original restaurants, where you can dine in heaven, was opened in 2006 and has been incredibly popular since the first days. At the moment there are similar restaurants in the other European cities, but Belgian dinner in the Sky remains the most popular and famous among them.

Despite the impressively high prices, the restaurant has never lacked the customer. To book the platform for a few hours, you must pay at least 20,000 US Dollars. On a special order, a platform next door can be raised, on which the piano is set up. The more frugal guests can dine with the violin. The second most populous restaurant of the network is in Vienna and was opened a few years ago. Dinner in the Sky is an excellent restaurant for those travelers who want to get hungry after new impressions and change their everyday life.

Montagne de Bueren

Montagne de Bueren (The Soldier's Staircase) is one of the main historical landmarks of the Belgian city of Liege. The staircase begins in the Or Chateau district and rises to a hill, where a fortress was located a few centuries ago. Today the park of the citadel is located here. This is a historical complex, which includes the surviving elements of construction and fortress walls. To see it, tourists need to go through 374 steps. The legendary Soldier's Staircase was built in 1875.

The story of the name of the staircase is quite unusual. In the 18th century there were a lot of entertainment and drinking places in the territory of the current quarter of Or Chateau. It was in these institutions that the soldiers from the fortress liked to rest. For them the stone staircase was the shortest route to long-awaited rest and fun. The purpose of the construction of the staircase was strategic. It was to allow the soldiers to quickly move to the center of the city if necessary.

Guests of Liege, who are not lazy to walk to the end of the stairs, will have an opportunity to admire not only unique historical sights. From the historic district, a wonderful panoramic view of the Maas river opens. Walking on the stairs will be comfortable and pleasant even for those who do not like long walks. On the stairs in certain places beautiful shops were established, where you can always relax. There is a cult place of interest in Liege with the official name "Buren Mount", it was named after the nobleman Vincent de Buren, who played an important role in the defense of the city.

Vogelenzangpark 17bis

Among the outstanding landmarks of Ghent is an original sculptural house with a complex name Vogelenzangpark 17bis, which was specially equipped for the opening of the TRACK: A Contemporary City Conversion festival. Located on a tree, the model of a small cottage is an exact copy of the building that is next to the tree. After the end of the art festival it has been decided to preserve it.

The author of the project of an unusual sculpture is an artist from Antwerp Benjamin Verdonck. Among the variety of urban buildings, he particularly liked the building of a retired club, which can be called a classic architectural monument of the mid-20th century. A beautiful historic building managed to survive to this day. In combination with an art monument, the old cottage looks very impressive. The only drawback of the house on a tree can be considered its modest size, it is too small to accommodate even one person in its walls.

The monument is no less popular. Every day curious tourists come here to take interesting photos. The impressive sculpture and the adjoining old building are surrounded by an incredibly beautiful park, through which you can stroll at any time of the year. Here grow majestic, old trees, in the shadow of which comfortable recreation zones have been equipped with benches, as well as other no less remarkable sculptures.

Mini-Europe

In Brussels, travellers have an opportunity to visit the most interesting "Mini Europe" park. It is located next to one of the most famous landmarks of the city the "Atomium" sculpture. It is believed, that it is in this park of miniatures that one can see some of the most upscale and expensive models in the world, which represent exact copies of the most important European landmarks at a scale of 1:25. The park has a lot of interactive layouts. Everywhere you can see trains running on miniature railways, windmill mills with rotating blades and even erupting Vesuvius.

The park was opened in 1989. Today its area is about 24000 square meters. On this extensive territory the most important sights of 27 European countries were presented. Here, you can see the Arc de Triomphe, the Basilica of Sacre-Coeur, and the Acropolis. You can also be photographed against the backdrop of the miniature Eiffel Tower and the Maestranza arena.

The park is famous not only for its variety of realistic miniatures, but also for its amazing landscape decorations. At its registration, beautiful lawn, various dwarf trees and bushes have been used. Enjoy this beauty is best of all in summer. According to approximate estimates, the Mini Europe miniature park is visited by about 375000 people annually. The annual income of the park is about three million euros. As a rule, tourists spend at least two hours on sightseeing. The park can be visited from early March to early January.

Chateau Miranda

In Belgium, travelers will have an opportunity to see one of the most beautiful empty castles in the world, Chateau Miranda. The last owners of this luxury castle were members of the Liedekerke Beaufort family. They were forced to leave their home in the Great French Revolution and moved to a neighboring farm. After the Second World War, the castle became the property of the national railway company, which has converted it into a camp for orphans.

Over the years, the cost of maintenance of the castle has been growing. In 1991, it has been finally abandoned due to lack of funding. Four years later, the historic building was seriously damaged by fire. At present, the Chateau Miranda officially belongs to the descendants of

Liedekerke Beaufort family. They have long been taken out all valuables, including precious elements of decoration. In recent years, castle owners received several offers to sale their property, as wealthy businessmen planned to convert it into a hotel.

None of the transactions took place. In fact, a few years ago current owners of the castle provided a formal requirement for its demolition. Many amazing legends are associated with the gracious building. Its history goes back for more than 800 years. According to the available historical records, during its existence, the fortification was taken by assault just once. The castle has witnessed many bloody battles. Despite the fact that the site was officially closed to the public, that does not stop visitors from the local community and tourists. Those who want to visit the Chateau Miranda, have to consider that the building is very dangerous, as it's destroying at our eyes.

Architecture and monuments

Architecture of Belgium. Must see and must visit landmarks

Atomium, Brussels

Interesting facts: » Atomium is another great attraction of Brussels. This building was constructed for the opening of the World Expo 1958; that's the symbol of the atomic age and the peaceful use of nuclear energy.

» Construction of the Atomium is decorated with nine atoms united in a root fragment of the crystal lattice of iron magnified 165 billion times.

» CNN called this building the most bizarre one in Europe.

» The height of the entire structure is 102 meters, and the weight of the structure is about 2,400 tons. The diameter of each of the nine areas of construction is 18 meters.

» Six areas are available for visit. In the mid-pipe of the building, connecting the central sphere there is an elevator. It's capable to lift the visitors to the restaurant and the viewing platform located in the highest ball of Atomium in 25 seconds.

Basilica of the Sacred Heart, Brussels

Interesting facts: » The Catholic Basilica of the Sacred Heart is dedicated to the Sacred Heart of Jesus. It was inspired by the eponymous basilica in Paris.

» This shrine is the sixth area of the Roman Catholic Church in the world.

» The church is the large structure with two towers and a green copper dome towering 89 meters above the ground. The length of the building is almost 165 meters.

» In total the church can accommodate up to 2,000 people.

» The basilica houses a restaurant, a Catholic radio station, theater, two museums, and a place of training cavers and climbers.

Brussels Town Hall, Brussels

Interesting facts: » The Brussels Town Hall is one of the most beautiful buildings in the city, which is the symbol of Brussels.

» The 5-meter statue of the Archangel Michael, the patron saint of Brussels, throwing devil is installed at the 96-meter Gothic Tower.

» The oldest part of the town hall was built in 1420, and the other part of the building was completed a little later (in 1450).

» Facade of the Hall is decorated with numerous statues of nobles, saints, and allegorical figures. In fact, existing sculpture are only reproductions, and originals are kept in the House of the King.

» The Town Hall is still used as the residence of the mayor and is available for tours.

Cathedral of St. Michael and St. Gudula, Brussels

Interesting facts: » The Cathedral of St. Michael and St. Gudula is one of the main attractions of Brussels, and the clearest example of Gothic architecture.

» The building of the cathedral is a symmetrical composition with two towers, within which there is a long staircase opening onto the terrace that is 64 meters high. The terrace offers a magnificent view of the city.

» The Cathedral has four doors decorated with wrought-reliefs and statues of saints. There is a huge stained glass above the main entrance.

» Stained glasses decorating the cathedral were created in the 16th century by Jan Haq and in 18-19th century by Jean-Baptiste Kaproner.

» The cathedral houses the mausoleum of the Belgian national hero Frederic de Merode.

Chapel Church, Brussels

Interesting facts: » The Chapel Church is one of the oldest churches in Brussels, the first mention of which dates back to 1134 year. During its long history the church has undergone many changes; it has repeatedly been destroyed and rebuilt.

» There are graves of local nobility and famous people inside the church.

» Nowadays, the Chapel Church is the parish church of the Polish Catholic community in Brussels.

» You can see the entire collection of paintings, sculptures and stained glass inside the temple.

» The church regularly hosts a variety of concerts. It's open to visitors all year round.

Church of Our Blessed Lady, Brussels

Interesting facts: » The Church of Our Blessed Lady is one of the clearest examples of temples built in the late Gothic style.

» The Church was built in the period from 1400 to 1594. It's located near Small Sablon Park that was laid in honor of the great men of the sixteenth century.

» The church building is decorated with beautiful stained glass windows; bright interior lighting is turned on in the night.

» Since its construction in 1784, the church has being serving as the burial place for noble aristocratic families.

» The church is famous for its numerous sculptures adorning the facade of the building, its grounds and interior.

Church of St. Catherine, Brussels

Interesting facts: » The building of the Church of St. Catherine was constructed in 1854-1874 years. Its facade combines Gothics with Romanesque features.

» The interior is very bright due to the white plaster on the walls; it's designed in neo-Renaissance style.

» The belfry standing apart from the temple is actually much older than the Church of St. Catherine. It has been preserved from the old church, which stood on that site previously.

» The main altar of the church is decorated with painting The Assumption of St. Catherine.

Halle Gate, Brussels

Interesting facts: » Halle Gate is the medieval gate and the only surviving fragment of the city wall of Brussels.

» Currently the building is used as a museum.

» The exact date of construction is unknown, but according to archival documents construction refers to the period between 1357 and 1373.

» In addition to defense and customs, in the 17th century the gate began to carry out the function of the prison.

» Currently gate is used as a branch of the Royal museums of Art and History. Exposition of the museum is devoted to the history of the gate itself, ancient weapons and Medieval history of Brussels.

La Monnaie, Brussels

Interesting facts: » La Monnaie has being among the leading European opera venues in recent decades.

» In 2011, La Monnaie was considered the best of the major opera houses.

» Festivals of theatrical performances and various creative competitions are often held there.

» Tours around the premises and theater workshops are held on Saturdays.

» The building of la Monnaie was built in 1855; that was the third construction for the theater. Auditorium houses 1,150 people, and the foyer is designed for 250 seats.

Law Courts, Brussels

Interesting facts:

» The Law Courts is the building of the state court in Brussels constructed between 1866 and 1883.

» Dimensions of the building are impressive: 160 meters long and 150 meters wide. The height of Law Courts reaches 142 meters.

» The Law Courts is the largest building constructed in the 19th century.

» Eight courtyards with a total area of 6,000 square meters, 27 large court rooms and 245 smaller courtrooms, and many other rooms are situated in the complex.

» The Law Courts is decorated with numerous sculptures of famous ancient lawyers, philosophers and orators such as Demosthenes, Lycurgus of Sparta, Cicero, Ulpian and others.

Royal Museum of Armed Forces, Brussels

Interesting facts:

» The Royal Museum of Armed Forces is the military history museum opened in 1923.

» The museum's collection is one of the largest military collections in the world.

» The museum has the separate pavilion of 100 meters long, which displays military aircrafts from the very first models of airplanes to modern jets. In addition, the museum even has a special tank yard.

» A lot of the exhibits are devoted to the first and second world wars.

» The museum has a huge collection of weapons, including cold and small arms, artillery, tanks, cars, planes, uniforms and equipment of the soldiers, and objects of military life. The museum also represents a variety of weapons dating back to the Middle Ages.

Royal Palace, Brussels

Interesting facts: » The Royal Palace is the official residence of the Belgian monarch situated in the heart of the capital.

» At present the royal family palace is used mainly as a venue for formal events.

» Every summer, the Royal Palace is traditionally open to the public. You can get inside the palace and see its galleries and chambers for free.

» Throne Hall with its grand decor, a wonderful mirror room, the ceiling of which is decorated with winged scarab beetles, and the Imperial Room with gorgeous golden flower pots, where plants of eleven colors, one for each province of Belgium, are the most notable places.

» The palace also houses the museum of Bellevue, which was once a hotel accommodating many famous people. Now that's the museum of history of Belgium.

Royal Palace of Laeken, Brussels

Interesting facts: » The Royal Palace of Laeken is the residence of the Belgian royal family, where it currently resides.

» The building of the palace was built in 1781-1785 in the style of

Classicism.

» The Royal Palace of Laeken is also famous for its territory boasting a magnificent park, a lake, the Royal Conservatory, a golf course and various pavilions.

» The park has two buildings unusual for Belgium style. Those are the Chinese pavilion and the Japanese tower that appeared here after Leopold II visited the World's Fair in Paris in 1900; there he saw pavilions of different countries, so he wanted to decorate his park.

» Opposite the park there is the neo-Gothic Church of Our Lady in Laeken with the crypt serving as the burial place of the royal family.

» Unfortunately, the palace itself is closed to the public, but the park, pavilions and conservatory are open for everyone.

Saint Jacques sur Coudenberg, Brussels

Interesting facts: » Saint Jacques sur Coudenberg was built in the second half of the 18th century in neoclassical style. It looks a lot like a palace or ancient Greek temple.

» The building is decorated with a wooden tower that serves as a belfry. It has four bells.

» Balustrades of the cathedral are decorated with three large statues; the statue of St. James can be seen in the center.

» Between French conquests the church was converted into a Temple of Reason, and later in the Temple of the Law. However, in 1802 it was re-consecrated as a Catholic.

» Today, Saint Jacques sur Coudenberg is the part of an ensemble of nine neoclassical buildings surrounding the perimeter of the Royal Square. The equestrian statue of Godefroid de Bouillon, who led the first Crusade, is in the center of the square.

Leisure and attractions

Attractions and nightlife

Active vacation in Belgium things to do, entertainment and nightlife

Small but hospitable, Belgium is all year round ready to offer its guests the opportunity to relax actively, cheerfully and with benefits. In the city of Peer, you can go skiing and snowboarding in the center of "Snow Valley" at any time of the year. Snow Valley is a large indoor building where it is always winter: there is a lot of real snow, there are artificial slopes for beginners and professionals, as well as a large flat area. This is a good place to have fun with the whole family. Sports shoes and skis can be rented, and after a walk in the snow, you can go to a cafe located right there. For those who wish to spend time in nature and have their mind blown away, it is worth going to the commune of Boussu, where "Natura Parc" is located. This is a rope town with a zipline and several levels of difficulty that will occupy visitors for several hours. In the municipality of Jalhay, there is an "AccroPark" where you can climb for a long time, up and down among lush greenery.

You can take a boat trip to Bruges, Ghent, Antwerp, Dinant, Zeebrugge, and Kinrooi. Depending on the city and company, tourists can choose between being in a group walk and conducting a private walk, a forty-minute ride or a few-hours tour, choose a holiday cruiser or a boat. They can also decide whether to rent a boat for themselves or employ the services of a guide. If you decide to take a ride along the canals and rivers of Belgium, you will get to see the country from a completely unexpected side and enjoy its nature and architecture. Professional guides will tell you a lot of interesting details about the culture and history of Belgium.

Relaxing on the water is fun and healthy. "Wavekarting" in Nieuwpoort offers a boat trip on the canal. In the municipality of Wachtebeke is located "Provinciaal domein Puyenbroeck" a large park for rest, slow walks, cycling (you can rent a bicycle), running and other activities. Here there is clean air and lots of greenery. You will also find fountains and a flower garden, which also serve as decoration for the Park. In addition, the Park has two swimming pools, a restaurant, a playground, and even places for camping and golfing. You can also go boating on the lake and chat with farm animals. It is better to visit the park on weekdays when there are fewer people in it.

You can dive under the water with a mask or scuba gear in the "TODI center" in Beringen. With the aid of modern equipment, you can conduct an absolutely safe swimming session in warm clear water among a really great variety of different shapes, sizes, and colors what could be more attractive for passionate diving enthusiasts? The professionalism and courtesy of instructors, a restaurant with a large selection of dishes, large locker rooms, swimming among the "sunken" cars, buildings and other items, will make your experience truly unforgettable. The Brussels' Center "Nemo 33" and "Transfo duiktank" in Zwevegem offer a similar experience of immersion in the safe and warm water of large indoor pools. Such an amusement will interest not only professionals and enthusiasts but also those who have never submerged under water.

Everyone dreams of going up in the sky in a balloon, but not everyone confesses. This activity is exciting and romantic, thus a great event for married people or love birds. Belgium will help you realize the dream of a wonderful, exciting flight. The "European Balloon Corporation" is located in Rhode-Saint-Genese, which provides clients with a wonderful experience of a safe flight over the beauties of Belgium. In addition to balloons, guests can fly a helicopter. "Bruges Ballooning" in Bruges allows you to look at the city from above, especially its ancient center, which is of course absolutely beautiful. You will definitely want to repeat this experience.

It is recommended for brave and thrill-seekers to go skydiving. For beginners, there is the opportunity of practicing flying in a wind tunnel, the safety of which is guaranteed by the "AIRSPACE Indoor

Skydiving" in Charleroi. Such an event will appeal to experienced skydivers. Another company that is ready to offer such an experience is "Fly-In" in the municipality of Grace-Hollogne. "RSRSpa" in Francorchamps is an opportunity not only to really jump with a parachute but also to take part in races on real race cars. In Suarlee, you can fly an airplane, performing aerobatic stunts with "Sensation Voltige".

Those that prefer walking and hiking are advised to go to Aywaille a great place to explore the nature of Belgium. Hills, streams, and forests give travelers vigor, thanks to the cleanliness and a huge amount of greenery. All you need are good shoes and a map or navigator. You can enjoy nature in "Stadspark" in Aalst. There is a lot of space here for walking and running. During the summer, musical performances are organized inside the Park. In the village of Nonceveux, travelers will find a beautiful valley, where it is good to walk among the trees, enjoy the closeness of water, the quietness and the clean air.

Parks and lanscapes

Nature of Belgium national parks and reserves for active recreation

Belgium is located in the western part of the European continent. It has shared borders with France, the Netherlands and Luxembourg. The north-western border of the country is washed by the North Sea.

The territory of the state is mainly represented by plains that become higher in the direction from the north-west to the south-east. The territory of Belgium can be divided into 3 natural landscape areas. In the northwestern part of the country, there is a sandy plain. In the center of Belgium lies a plateau, which is a hilly area. In the southeast of the country, the Ardennes Mountains begin, smoothly moving into the territory of neighboring France. In the Ardennes is to be found the highest point in Belgium Mount Botranzh, which is 694 meters in height. More than half the area of Belgium is set aside for farming. About 20% of the Belgian territory is occupied by forests. An extensive network of rivers is connected by numerous channels. They are convenient for shipping, as they are not covered by ice during the winter due to the moderately warm maritime climate.

The Zwin Nature Reserve is located near the border with the Netherlands. It is spread over an area of 1.5 square kilometers. The reserve is located on the site where shallow sea bay used to be. Today it is a whole range of marshes and salt marshes. Founded in 1952, Zwin was simply a paradise for birds. The marshland is chosen by about 100 species of birds for nesting. Tourists not only from Belgium but also from many European countries come to see the birds in their natural habitat. The best time to visit Zwin is in spring when the nesting period is around the corner. Only 30% of the reserve's territory is open to visitors. Walking in Zwin is possible only along special paths, so as not to disturb the unique eco-environment.

One of the pieces of Belgian nature undisturbed by man is the "High Marsh" national nature reserve. Founded in 1957, this reserve is today the largest in the state. Its high marsh can be seen stretching over the eastern border of the country. The task of creating a reserve was to ensure the protection of the plateau and the preservation of tender bogs' ecosystems as well as the fauna representatives inhabiting them.

The entire territory of the reserve is covered with marshes and peatlands. Due to Peat moss growing here, which becomes peat over time, the high marsh has created an ideal environment for a comfortable habitat for many unique plants and ferns. Some fens are over 10 thousand years old. During the winter period, the slopes of the reserve turn into one of the country's best ski resorts. Visitors are only allowed to stroll through the reserve on foot. Nevertheless, the local tourism center offers ski rentals in winter, and bicycles or horses in the warm season.

The first national park Hoge Kempen, which was opened in 2006 in Flanders, is a special pride of the Belgians. Its territory covers the land of 6 municipalities and is about 5000 hectares. The entire reserve is composed of pine forests that grow interspersed with green meadows. The place where sand and gravel were mined previously has now become an impressive lake, remarkable in size. All the beauty of the park can be seen by rising to the natural heights of Hoge Kempen, which is a little less than 100 meters. The reserve has become a habitat for such rare animals as a slippery snake, European bee wolf or antlions. You will also come across a roe here. You can have a view of the most beautiful places in the national park by going for a walk along one of the hiking routes. Their length is varied and ranges from 3 to 14 kilometers. In specialized stalls, there is an opportunity to buy a map, on which walking or cycling routes have been marked.

On the North Sea coast in the town of Koksijde, there is a nature reserve called Hoge Blekker. It covers an area of 18 hectares. The highlights of the reserve are sand dunes, each of which has its own name. The reserve itself is named after the largest dune on the entire Belgian coast. It goes as high as 33 meters into the sky. Many dunes in the reserve have an impressive age. The time of their formation has been recorded to be the period between the 16th and 19th centuries. The dunes have a horseshoe shape, elongated in the direction of the wind. You will find various crops growing between the dunes. This became possible due to the use of fish chitling as fertilizer by local farmers. To prevent the dunes from expanding into the surrounding islands, various shrubs and low trees were planted around the perimeter. On the territory of Hoge Blekker is grown elderberry, blackthorn, hawthorn, and sea buckthorns. You can walk around the reserve at any time, but only along special paths. Separate routes have been equipped for tourists who wish to move around on bicycles.

Soul of Belgium

Cuisine and restaurants

National cuisine of Belgium for gourmets. Authentic recipes, delicacies and specialties
Belgian traditional cuisine was significantly influenced by the cuisines of Germany, the Netherlands, and France. Everyone must have heard about the magnificent Belgian chocolate, as well as the wonderful waffles and beer. Nevertheless, there are lots of dishes in the national cuisine that are also tasty and worth trying by everyone at least once in their life. Popular dishes in Belgium vary from region to region, but the basis of Belgian dishes customarily consists of asparagus, bread, potatoes, cabbage, tomatoes, chicken and rabbit meat, and when it comes to seafood, they prefer such an exotic dish as sea snails. According to some reports, everyone's favorite potato fries originated precisely from Belgium. Belgians prefer ketchup to mayonnaise. Portions of dishes here are always large and satisfying.

Meat of periwinkle can be bought from street vendors in Belgium. Another popular meal from seafood is shrimps. They are often eaten with a few glasses of beer. They are usually filled with tomatoes or added to vegetable salads, mixed with mayonnaise. There is also the tender eel meat, stewed in herbs, which is eaten hot. The unusual combination of meatballs and cherries will delight any gourmet: meatballs are served in cherry sauce, with whole seedless cherries. In Belgium, residents also love meat rolls, boiled or roasted rabbit meat, chicken soup, and beef stew. Let us not forget to mention the Belgian cheeses, which are great in both number and variety. They differ from each other in tastes, hardness, as well as in the method of preparation. Sheep, Cow, Goat and Buffalo Milk are used in the preparation of these cheeses. However different, they all possess a characteristic excellent quality.

Although Belgian cuisine is not vegetarian, as it is almost entirely made of meat and seafood, the locals eat quite a lot of vegetables. Asparagus, especially the white one, is very popular in Belgium. White asparagus has a more delicate flavor. When boiled, it is added to many dishes, especially those that contain eggs or salmon, making the food even more satisfying. Sometimes white asparagus is added even in desserts, for example, in ice cream. The Belgians love "Stoemp"; mashed potatoes mixed with vegetables. Carrots, potatoes, leeks are added to meat dishes, while fruits can be found in many desserts. Potato soup is also quite popular.

Belgians often eat sweet bread for breakfast, sometimes replacing it with raisin bread. Chocolates made in Belgium are known all over the world for their high quality. You will find here, tiles of white, dark and milk chocolate with raisins, orange, mint, nuts, rum, cookies, caramel; sets of chocolate sweets in the form of hearts, shells with various fillings and milk and coffee flavor; praline, hot chocolate. Belgium can therefore without exaggeration be called a chocolate country. Waffles are eaten with caramel, ice cream, vanilla, whipped cream, or fruit, sometimes without supplement. They are used as a dessert and as a snack.

In the middle of the day, many Belgians like to drink beer, and at dinner, it is common to drink some traditional strong Genever. With regards to soft drinks, residents of Belgium drink tea, coffee, soda, juices, milk, and milkshakes. On holidays in the country, special donuts are eaten, which are called "Oliebollen". During the winter holidays, these sweets with powdered sugar on top are sold at every corner. At Christmas, they eat goose, turkey or lamb, mussels, apples, peaches, and cherries, as well as a variety of sweets bought at the Christmas market. The cake roll "Yule log" is an absolute must-have on any table.

The table etiquettes in Belgium are not much different from the rules of dining etiquette in other European countries. It is customary to hold your hands on the table, avoiding putting your elbows on it. Putting your hands on your knees is considered inappropriate. Guests do not have to choose places at the table on their own as they will be seated by the host. More often, the spouses are seated separately. All food on a plate must be eaten. Alcohol offered by the host should be accepted. In a cafe or restaurant, waiters are called either with a raised hand or an eye contact, snapping of the fingers and screaming is considered uncultured. You cannot use a toothpick being at the table. For this, you need to retire to the bathroom having apologized. And of course, you cannot get into your mouth with your fingers, pick your teeth with a knife or fork.

Tourists wishing to visit Belgian catering places are advised to go to the bakery in Brussels, "Charli", which has been pleasing visitors wonderfully for almost ten years with superb coffee and remarkably fresh pastries. All this you can enjoy on a neat table, and in a relaxed atmosphere. The metropolitan "Cafe Velvet" is famous for Colombian coffee, milkshakes, sweet cakes, and excellent service. In Bruges, there is a traditional Belgian cuisine restaurant "Belgian Pigeon House". It consists of a bar and a small underground restaurant. Meals here are served like real Belgian portions, so it is best to come here on an empty stomach.

Traditions and lifestyle

National traditions of Belgium. Habits, mentality and the way of living

Belgium is divided into three parts. Most of the Belgian population is Flemish, who lives in the northern part of the country and speaks Dutch dialects. Walloons on the other hand, live in the southern part and speak Walloon and French. The northeast is inhabited by native German speakers. Dutch and French are the official languages of the country. No matter how evident the tension between the Flemish and the Walloons is in terms of political views, all Belgians are quite tolerant, polite and uncomplicated people and do not like to sort out their differences by taking the law into their hands. Most Belgians call themselves Catholics. Nevertheless, during religious celebrations and rites such as weddings and baptisms, almost everyone in Belgium, including non-religious citizens, come together to participate.

Belgians love comfort and safety and absolutely do not tolerate it when the quality of goods and services offered to them is poor or substandard. Therefore, it is difficult to find a restaurant, store or hotel in the whole country that would not offer high-quality service. Food and drinks for the Belgian should always be the best. Residents of Belgium love schedules; they often adjust their lives to pre-scheduled dates. The Belgians do not like when something that has been planned goes wrong, and also, deviation from the plan can upset them. They cannot, therefore, be called unpredictable. A Belgian will come to a scheduled meeting a little earlier or, which happens less often, by the designated time. Even a slight delay in Belgium is a sign of disrespect.

Family for the Belgians always comes first. Residents of Belgium do not like to move and often live in one place all their lives. This leads to the fact that often all family members, including distant relatives, live nearby. A Belgian would rather spend several hours on the way to and from work every day rather than move closer to his place of work. Typically, residents of Belgium marry at 18-20 years. Most of the men and women from 30 who are still single are mostly divorced. In recent years, the age of entering into marriage has increased, and the number of divorcees has also increased. On average, two children are born in families. Women rarely change their names upon getting married.

Belgians are not lovers of change; they do not like to change their social circle. They feel most comfortable at home among relatives or friends. Therefore, it is not so easy to start a friendship with the Belgians. Residents of Belgium are usually tolerant towards members of other nationalities, races, religions, and sexual affinities. A rather large percentage of Belgians are dissatisfied with their country. This nation can be called the least nationalistic the people of Belgium often criticize the government, the weather, as well as the culture of their country. Moreover, each Belgian is proud of his home, constantly keeps it in a clean state, and cares for the garden. Many Belgian citizens sweep the street in front of their houses.

The people of Belgium are very tidy and clean. Their homes, cars, cities, clothes, public places always appear clean and shining. Belgians, in general, attach great importance to their appearance, which must be borne in mind by guests of the country who want to impress new Belgian friends or business partners. The citizens of Belgium pay much attention to their appearance and expect the same from their fellow citizens and tourists. The Belgian will not allow himself to leave the house without making sure that his clothes are perfectly clean and fit well. They do not like negligence, lack of punctuality, carelessness and irresponsibility in themselves and others, and consider good manners and good breeding to be important.

Residents of Belgium enjoy chatting with close friends at a dinner table at home or in a restaurant. New acquaintances are not invited into the house immediately as such an important step takes time. Belgians do not discuss their or other people's personal lives with anyone other than close relatives and friends. In this case, the Belgians can start a romantic relationship abruptly, for example, after the first date. When meeting with strange and unfamiliar people, a handshake is usually expected. People who were well known to one another replace it (the handshake) with three kisses on the cheeks (only a woman with a woman or a man with a woman), while kind of kissing the air next to her, not the cheek.

Belgians may appear cold, unemotional and closed to foreigners. However, in fact, they can be romantic, as well as lovers of being bothered and complaining about something and this is when the Belgians are extra emotional. Those who want to make friends with the Belgians will have to show patience, but it is worth it because only to close people do they truly express what is in their hearts. In general, the people of Belgium are modest, do not brag about wealth, achievements, appearance, intellect and other things, and do not tolerate it from others. They do not like to waste money and time, and they are hardworking people. It is therefore easy and pleasant to do business with them.

Accommodation

Stylish hotels

Stylish weekend in Belgium collection of top boutique-hotels

Belgium could not avoid such fashionable directions as design hotels. Modern fashion trends can be traced in a number of hotels offering their guests a variety of interesting solutions through the provision of accommodation services. The atmosphere of the capital of Belgium offers you the opportunity to appreciate the design hotel Home & the City. The hotel's convenient location which is within walking distance to the historic center of the city has become another of its advantage. All hotel rooms are decorated in a stylish way with original solutions. Each room has a toilet and a bathroom, television, and Wi-Fi. In the city of Antwerp is situated a boutique hotel, Small Luxury & Boutique De Witte Lelie. This place has only 10 rooms, but high ceilings with crossbars and a spiral staircase give it a special charm. Each room is decorated in a unique style and color. The hotel is located near the central city squares and the main shopping street, Meir.

Den Witten Leeuw, Brugge

Many popular hotels in Bruges are located in historic buildings. Den Witten Leeuw is no exception. It is also open in an eye-catching building with centuries-old history. This hotel is very popular with couples, who enjoy staying in one of the three beautiful twin rooms with romantic design. Large white beds with canopies, posh textiles, genuine antiquities and artworks are the main design elements of this magnificent hotel. Many original decorations have been preserved in the hotel, such as historic beam joints and mansard ceilings.

Royal Windsor Hotel Grand Place, Brussels

Exclusive design in royal style has become one of the main peculiarities and advantages of posh Royal Windsor Hotel Grand Place. Its guestrooms feature an eye-catching design with rare materials used premium sorts of wood and elegant antique furniture. Twin rooms feature large bedrooms with canopies, and some guestrooms have several functional zones separated by draping. All rooms are decorated with branded textiles, genuine artworks and vintage accessories. Public zone of the hotel come with authentic antique furniture.

For Four Flat, Gent

The historic center of Ghent is home to one more quality apartment hotel, For Four Flat. This place is also distinguished by creative design.

The inner premises are mostly made in white with some bright accents, such as flower bouquets and paintings with beautiful landscapes. The natural beauty of the rooms is underlined by light wood furniture. Thanks to large panoramic windows, all guestrooms at For Four Flat look airy and are well lit. It is also worth mentioning a state-of-art lighting system, plasma TVs, iPod dock stations, and a small kitchen with all amenities in the rooms. The hotel's roof has been turned into a spacious terrace with panoramic views of the Saint Bavo Cathedral and other important historic landmarks of Ghent.

De Keyser Hotel, Antwerpen

One more wonderful hotel is located just a few steps away from the main railway station. De Keyser Hotel is located in a grandiose historic building. The outside look of the building is quite strict and modest, but inside guests will find charming atmosphere and modern design made mostly in beige shades. Floors in guestrooms come with lightwood parquet. Inside there are large white beds, black curtains and modern lightning with black lamp-shades. All guestrooms are decorated with beautiful paintings and a sophisticated conditioning system. Some guestrooms feature marble bathrooms.

Maison Bousson, Brugge

Fans of modern style may be fond of Maison Bousson mini hotel. It is located not far from the centre of Bruges and is open on the site of a former quarry. The hotel has only three guest rooms made in light shades and decorated with designer furniture and interesting artworks. Besides standard paintings, one can see various colorful textiles, interesting collages, handmade items and elegant vases with flowers. The design hotel

Aloft Brussels Schuman, Brussels

Aloft Brussels Schuman was the first hotel in Europe operating under the Aloft brand. This is a modern hotel targeted at young travellers, so it features catchy design and many socializing options. Quite spacious rooms with very high ceilings of up to three meters are made in the open space manner, and furniture is used to separate one functional zone from another. Aloft promises luxurious style at a reasonable price, so this hotel will be a wonderful choice for all travellers.

Design B&B Logidenri, GentAffordable

Design B&B Logidenri is also distinguished by a very creative look and rooms planning. Beautiful stone and wood décor, open space bathroom with panoramic windows and beautiful garden views, interesting panels that imitate a fireplace guests of Design B&B Logidenri can stay in a modern designer hotel and don't run out of the budget. A daily continental breakfast with a wide choice of fresh fruit and homemade baking will be a worthy addition to the pleasant stay at this hotel.

B&B De Bijloke, Gent

Budget travelers are not deprived of an opportunity to stay in a creative designer hotel in Ghent. They are recommended to take a look at B&B De Bijloke. This hotel is open in a beautiful townhouse and offers only three guest rooms. All the rooms are made in different styles, and every room features beautiful décor and accessories made of wood and a big comfortable bed with elegant bed clothing. Besides an interesting design, it's worth mentioning a well-groomed inner yard with a garden with comfortable benches and sun protection roofs.

Hotel Firean, Antwerpen

Hotel Firean is owned by the Iserbyt family. The hotel is often called the most charming hotel in whole Belgium and is well-known beyond the borders of the country. It is distinguished by its outstanding architectural style that is a wonderful combination of cozy classics and antiquity. Owners of the hotel do everything to maintain this special atmosphere and make sure guests are pleased.

Charme Hotel Hancelot, Gent

Charme Hotel Hancelot offers tourists to make a tour to the past centuries. This hotel is open in a luxurious mansion that once belonged to a noble baron. The building was carefully restored in order to save the atmosphere of the past. Guest rooms and public spaces feature antique furniture, and high ceilings add special aristocratic charm to the hotel. Massive glass chandeliers and giant mirrors, elegant tables and cabinets made of dark wood all these accents remind of the culture of the past. There is a wonderful hall with a TV and fireplace at Charme Hotel Hancelot, which is an amazing place for a big company.

Luxury hospitality

Where to stay in Belgium most luxurious and fashionable hotels

Gand The capital of the European Union simply cannot afford not to have luxury hotels in its own square, especially considering the constant influx of tourists and business class guests who constantly visit this country and are accustomed to the highest level of comfort. Practically in the center of the Belgian capital is the luxury Tangla Hotel Brussels which is very popular among tourists. Polite staff will put in every effort to ensure comfortable living conditions for their own guests. The rooms have their own lounge, free Wi-Fi, television, and mini-bar. The hotel has a restaurant and a fitness center. The convenient location in the center of Brugge has made the 5-star luxury Hotel Dukes' Palace one of the best in its class. The almost homely furnishings and design of the rooms allow guests to feel at home in it. Guests, if desired, without leaving the hotel, can visit a swimming pool, spa, restaurant or bar. The hotel has the possibility of holding business conferences using its own business center.

NH Gent Sint Pieters, Gent

NH Gent Sint Pieters show on the map is open in a magnificent building of Renaissance style. Every traveler will easily find a room to fit his/her taste at NH Gent Sint Pieters. There are charming rooms in retro style and stylish modern rooms with creative photographic wallpapers and designer furniture. Every morning, a premium breakfast with fresh sweet baking and fruit waits for guests of the hotel. Among other advantages of the hotel, it is worth noting its convenient location close to SMAK Museum and ICC Business Center.

Stanhope Hotel, Brussels
Stanhope Hotel show on the map was the first five-star hotel in Belgium. The design of the magnificent hotel is reminiscent of a prestigious residence in the classic English style. Elegant premium furniture, exclusive flower pattern textiles, amazing painting and Chinese white and blue vases make the hotel look very solid and posh. The hotel also features a picturesque garden with a fountain, and charming bar and restaurant designed like a royal banquet hall and decorated with busts of members of royal families. One can always hear classic music in the hall of the hotel.

Holiday Inn Gent Expo, Gent
The luxurious Holiday Inn Gent Expo show on the map is located not far from Flanders Expo Exhibition Complex. This hotel is popular with fans of different types of rest. Besides classic rooms with modern furniture, the hotel features a range of extra services. Fans of Belgian cuisine should not forget to visit Atrium restaurant that is famous for a huge choice of national treats and signature dishes. Atrium bar serves a variety of popular sorts of Belgian beer and wine. Guests are welcome to mix their gastronomic feast with visits to a fitness center or bicycle rides.

Ramada Plaza Antwerp, Antwerpen

Business travelers might prefer Ramada Plaza Antwerp show on the map as it is located right in the heart of the business district of the city. The hotel occupies a part of a modern skyscraper with panoramic windows. Elegant guestrooms are made mostly in caramel and coffee shades, and long term guests will be pleased with comfortable serviced apartments. Guests of the hotel can use sauna and gym every day free of charge. There is also a stylish night club in the building. Travellers, who prefer to spend their evenings in a more relaxed way, are welcome in Hugo's restaurant, which windows offer panoramic views of Hertogenpark.

Le Plaza, Brussels

The design of hotel Le Plaza show on the map was inspired by the famous Parisian hotel George V. Inner décor of the hotel is no less refine and elegant than its French paragon. Antique furniture, crystal chandeliers, marble floors and expensive carpets create the elegant style of the '30s of the previous century. There are some antique areas at the hotel, such as the theater hall with unique décor in the Mauritian style. Sticking to traditions of aristocratic luxury, the hotel, nevertheless, harmoniously combines them with modern comfort.

Hotel de Flandre, Gent

The next hotel in the list is particularly popular with fans of excursions. Hotel de Flandre show on the map is open in a beautiful 18th-century building. Among its attractive advantages, it's worth mentioning the unique décor of guest rooms made of natural materials and fabrics. Massive wooden ceilings with built-in lamps, beam cedarwood and a fireplace in every guest room, old sculptures, and comfortable furniture the charming atmosphere of the hotel is one of its main secrets of popularity. In the morning, the hotel offers a buffet type breakfast, and in the evening everyone is welcome to relax in the comfortable lounge and try best sorts of Belgian wine.

Hyllit Hotel, Antwerpen

Many upscale guests of Antwerp choose to stay at Hyllit Hotel show on the map that is located in the heart of the Diamond Quarter. Guests of the hotel are welcome to book magnificent luxury rooms and suites with king size beds and exclusive tapestries. One of the best restaurants in the city, Gran Duca, is also located in the hotel and occupies its top floor and terrace. In this restaurant travelers can try best dishes of Italian and French cuisine, as well as wonderful wine. The hotel's spa offers a wide range of treatments, some of which are free for guests.

Grand Hotel Casselbergh, Brugge

Elegant Grand Hotel Casselbergh show on the map is located in three medieval buildings. The face of the hotel features original decorations that date back to the 13th and 16th centuries. The hotel's design is mostly classical, very elegant and contains many antique details. Luxurious rooms feature beautiful views of the canal. The hotel's lounge zone is not only a good place to pamper yourself with delicious light snacks and drinks; it's a magnificent historic place with a fireplace and a library. Fans of ultimate comfort and prestigious places will like Grand Hotel Casselbergh as it is often called the most prestigious hotel in whole Bruges.

Ghent Marriott Hotel, Gent
Korenlei Quay is the location of the prestigious Ghent Marriott Hotel show on the map, which outstanding quality will please even most discerning guests. Rooms of the hotel are distinguished by large size, panoramic floor-to-ceiling windows, and luxurious king size beds. The hotel has a fitness center and a stylish lobby area made in black and white, which is perfect for relaxation. The hotel's restaurant is worth a separate mention panoramic windows, live music on evenings, and delicious modern Belgian cuisine are among its advantages.

Crowne Plaza Antwerpen, Antwerpen
A no less striking and prestigious place, Crowne Plaza Antwerpen show on the map is a great hotel that will leave even hard-to-please guests satisfied. One of the best wellness centres in the city, Octopus, is located in the hotel and all of its guests are welcome to use its marvelous swimming pool free of charge. On a paid basis, travelers can enjoy various types of sauna, massage rooms and a modern gym. In the evening, head to ANNA lounge bar, where guests are offered to try the most delicious dishes of Flemish cuisine.

Hotels with history

Preserved history of Belgium: long-standing and ancient hotels

Sint-Petrus-en-Pauluskerk The Belgians, living in a country rich in history, not only maintain their own history but also try to extract a lot of benefits from it. Historical buildings have been long adapted for hotels, which also turned out to be in no way inferior, but sometimes superior to modern hotels in terms of comfort. In a house built in 1930, which survived the most terrible war in the history of mankind, is the B & B hotel. Just some walking distance from it is the elite district of Brussels, Ixelles. You will find located near the hotel, the Flagey square, sophisticated bars, and a concert hall. Functionality and modern amenities both combine to create a pleasant atmosphere of fun and relaxation here. The Kempinski Hotel Dukes' Palace in Bruges is located in a 15th-century building that previously housed the Prinsenhof Castle. The interiors of the hotel are richly decorated with images and ornaments from the dawn of the castle. Today, the hotel offers a spa, fitness center, bar and swimming pool to its guests.

Place 2 stay, Gent

A miniature old building, the look and décor of which are in line with classic national traditions, has become home for Place 2 stay show on the map. This hotel offers only 7 comfortable apartments with elegant design and clean lines, which still keep the atmosphere of past centuries. Some rooms come with small balconies with stone fencing.

Guests will admire these balconies since they feature a magnificent panoramic view of St-Braafs Square. Large windows of different shapes allow much of daylight in, while the presence of modern electronics makes a stay at Place 2 Stay hotel very comfortable. Independent travelers will be pleased with a fully equipped kitchen with tableware, an oven, and a microwave.

Hotel Firean, Antwerpen

Hotel Firean show on the map is a family run small hotel that has become famous far beyond the borders of the city thanks to its one-of-a-kind historic design. The building of the hotel, which is a marvelous example of the art deco style, was built in 1929. The building belongs to the Iserbyt family, who decided to transform a posh mansion into a hotel in 1986. During more than 30 years the hotel has been providing the best service for its guests. The magnificent hotel has only 9 guestrooms decorated with precious antique items. All the rooms have different design, so a stay at this hotel will never be boring.

Vakantie Logies Hollywood, Brugge

Vakantie Logies Hollywood show on the map is one of the most interesting historic hotels in Bruges. As it is not hard to guess from its name, the hotel's design is dedicated to Hollywood. It is located in a typical historic building with the preserved original wooden carcass. Besides antique furniture, the hotel exhibits an interesting collection of vintage photographs. In the photos, you will see Hollywood stars of the middle of the 20th century, retro filmmaking equipment and interesting on set moments. When it's warm outside, guests of this wonderful hotel are welcome to relax on an open terrace, where they will be treated with best sorts of Belgian beer.

Hotel Noga, Brussels

A charming house not far from the old fishing market of St. Catherine has become home for Hotel Noga show on the map. A team of talented designers worked hard to create a warm and pleasant atmosphere of the middle of the 20th century. Walls in rooms are covered with cute vintage wallpapers and feature colorful textiles carefully selected in accordance with trends of the past. Many rooms and public zones are decorated with interesting vintage items beautiful furniture, paintings, ship models, hand-painted vases and lamps, antique carpets and other interesting accessories that will certainly draw the attention of history fans.

Best Western Residence Cour St Georges, Gent

The historical part of Ghent is home to one more amazing hotel, Best Western Residence Cour St Georges show on the map, that is open in a grandiose 18th-century building. Its guest rooms are mostly made in elegant colors, and some rooms still have the original arched ceilings. Convenient location remains one of the main attractive points of the historical hotel. The famous Huis van Alijn Museum, Gravensteen Castle, and St. Nicolas Church are located just a couple of minutes away from the hotel. Every morning, a hearty breakfast is served for hotel guests. The breakfast includes numerous national delicacies and fresh baking.

Erasmus Hotel, Gent

Erasmus Hotel show on the map is open in a unique 16th-centry building with carefully preserved original elements of décor. Spiral stairs with high wooden banisters, amazing fireplaces, and antique furniture, crystal chandeliers, historical candelabras and clocks the design of Erasmus Hotel is reminiscent of a museum of history. There is even a charming ancient garden that is still decorated with original landscape compositions.

The Pand, Brugge

The Pand show on the map is another wonderful historic hotel, which is located in an 18th-century mansion. The family, which owns the hotel, is keen on art, so the refined taste of the owners has reflected in design and atmosphere of the hotel. Romantic guestrooms come with large beds with canopies, premium textiles, antique furniture, and are decorated with valuable artworks. A peaceful inner yard with a charming fountain, a library with a great collection of old books, a wonderful bar the atmosphere of elegance and comfort reigns throughout the hotel. On demand of travelers, fine breakfasts on silver tableware and premium champagne can be served directly in guestrooms.

Hotel Gravensteen, Gent

Hotel Gravensteen show on the map is open in a beautiful building that belongs to the middle of the 19th century. Only several steps separate the building from the same named building. Guests of Hotel Gravensteen find will peaceful relaxation in the atmosphere of luxury and comfort. In the morning, the stylish salon is used to serve buffet type breakfast for guests. The beautifully furnished bar of the hotel is an ideal place for trying delicious Belgian beer that is always offered with a wide choice of different signature snacks. The historical hotel is surrounded by a lush garden with centuries-old trees and magnificent flowerbeds.

B&B The Baron, Antwerpen
The luxury Baroque style town house, which was built in 1860, was transformed into B&B The Baron show on the map hotel. Its luxurious rooms made in retro style are simply stunning with their antique wallpapers, authentic historic furniture and precious artworks throughout the hotel. Guestrooms for couples are very charming and romantic as they have king size beds with valance, old paintings and finest china. Public zones are no less wonderful as the hotel's owners managed to keep the original décor, high ceiling with fretwork and carved columns.

NH Brugge, Brugge
With its original stained-glass windows, brick fireplaces and old beam ceilings, historic NH Brugge show on the map resembles a 17th-century monastery. Guestrooms are mostly made in French

countryside style. The stone terrace of the hotel is an ideal place to have a cup of coffee in the morning or relax and enjoy a delicious cocktail in the evening. The hotel's staff is very friendly, hospitable and tries to do their best to make sure guests feel comfortable and are pleased with their stay at NH Brugge

Famous hotels

Legends of Belgium famous hotels renowned by history

Hotels, like any other buildings and structures, can become famous and iconic buildings not only for their own guests but also for residents of the country. In Belgium, there are a number of hotels that have long become famous far beyond the borders of the country. Hotel Jan Brito is housed in a building which was formerly the residence of Baroness de Giey in Bruges. Interiors of rooms are saturated with old-world atmosphere, decorated in styles of different eras. Inside the hotel is a garden that has remained untouched, so that its age now dates far back to the Renaissance period. It has growing in it, a 100-year-old beech tree. Holidays in this luxury hotel will leave the most pleasant memories. In the Belgian castle of Château d'Hassonville, built in ancient times as a hunting lodge for King Louis XIV, today is a famous hotel. In the castle, there is a popular gourmet restaurant. You are sure to have a great time in its estate of 55 hectares.

B&B Azur Beauty & Wellness, Gent

Travelers, who prefer to have not only an interesting but also a healthy vacation, are recommended to take a look at B&B Azur Beauty & Wellness. Besides beautiful rooms made with dominating white color, the hotel offers services of its high-class wellness center. Inside, travelers will find several types of sauna, a large rest area with hydro massage baths, and a tropical shower. Visitors can attend healing massage sessions or visit a cosmetologist. The wellness center is made in an oriental style that makes relaxation there even more unusual.

Hotel Orion, Gent

Tourist groups and travelers with children usually praise Hotel Orion show on the map that is open in a beautiful villa that dates back to the beginning of the 20th century. The variety of guest rooms is simply amazing, so both single travelers and large groups will find a suitable room there. The modern design of guest rooms is worth a separate mention. The rooms are made in black and white, while bathrooms feature a combination of red and white colors. Modern electronics completes the inimitable designer style. Other amenities include a swimming pool, saunas, and a charming garden with furnished terraces.

Relais & Châteaux Hotel Heritage, Brugge

Travellers, who find the idea of living in a hotel with rich history appealing, are recommended to pay attention to Relais & Châteaux Hotel Heritage. This hotel is located in a magnificent building constructed in 1869. Initially, the building belonged to one of rich inhabitants of Bruges. Later, the building was transformed into a bank and nowadays it's a hotel with 22 unique guestrooms that would suite even a king. Giant beds with crispy white blankets, carpets with interesting patterns, old paintings in heavy frames, crystal chandeliers you will see valuable antiques simply everywhere in this amazing hotel. By the way, there is a 14th-century wine cellar at the hotel, which has survived from the original building.

Hotel Castel, Gent
Hotel Castel show on the map is equally liked by active rest fans, comfort devotees, and travelers who cannot imagine a single day in Belgium without drinking the magnificent local beer. The hotel is conveniently located close to Gent-Sint-Pieters railway station, allowing guests to travel freely in the territory of the city and its suburbs. The popular hotel is famous for one of the best beer restaurants in the city, where visitors can choose from more than 150 sorts of the popular drink and enjoy various locally produced meat delicacies.

Hotel Jan Brito, Brugge
The former residence of baroness de Geiy is now known as Hotel Jan Brito show on the map. The building of the hotel is protected by UNESCO, so all restorations were very thoughtful and their main aim was to keep the original design and look of the building. Travelers are welcome to admire the beauty of antique marble fireplaces, paintings and the oak ladder. Guestrooms feature the style of different epochs,

but all of them reflect the atmosphere of the past. While at the hotel, don't forget to visit a romantic inner yard of Renaissance period and a hundred-year-old beech that grows there. Despite its historic look, Hotel Jan Brito is a luxurious hotel with modern services.

Novotel Gent Centrum, Gent

Novotel Gent Centrum show on the map is a stylish and reasonably priced resort type hotel. In order to organize an interesting and diversified holiday, one doesn't necessarily need to leave the hotel's territory. Novotel Gent Centrum features a wonderful swimming pool with terraces, which is surrounded by dense exotic plants. Sports fans will be pleased with a quality gym, and the best way to end the day is to relax in a comfortable sauna at Novotel. The hotel's bar with an interior garden is a marvelous place for a romantic dinner the choice of drinks and signature treats is simply flawless.

ibis Gent Centrum Opera, Gent

The charming ibis Gent Centrum Opera show on the map has been very popular with guests of Ghent for many years. It is regularly chosen by active youth and mature people as a place for their vacation. ibis Gent Centrum Opera has a ton of advantages and location is one of them the hotel is open near the Vlaamse Opera and Sint Baafskathedraal, and it takes only several minutes to reach the popular shopping mall Gent Zuid by foot. The décor of guestrooms is made in a classic style and in mostly pastel colors, while the design of public spaces simply strikes visitors with the abundance of bright colors and designer accessories. There is a stylish bar at the hotel, and in the morning a delicious buffet type breakfast is served for guests of the hotel.

Kempinski Hotel Dukes Palace, Brugge

Kempinski Hotel Dukes Palace show on the map is located in a fully restored palace of the 15th century. The palace was built by Philip the Good, the Duke of Burgundy specifically for his marriage ceremony with Isabel de Aragon. Magnificent interior of the palace is made mostly in bold violet, bronze and green shades that can be found on ancient tapestries and only underline the glorious past of the building. Gardens of the palace are no less breath-taking with their ancient sculptures by famous masters. Elegance in every detail only proves that this historic place is worth the highest praise.

Romantic hotels

Romantic hotels in Belgium best places for intimate escape, wedding or honeymoon

Casa Romantico, Brugge

Villa-hotel Casa Romantico show on the map is an ideal place for couples who seek privacy and serenity. This hotel is also open in a beautiful historic building and is surrounded by a lush garden. Besides charming guestrooms, guests of the hotel are welcome to rest in a cozy inner yard with wooden terraces and an outdoor swimming pool. The guestrooms look slightly different, but all of them feature beautiful handmade wooden furniture and premium textiles. The most unusual room is located on the mansard and has beautiful beam ceiling. Finally, there is a nice bar at the hotel, which is a great place in the evening.

The Dominican, Brussels
Only a short walk separates Grand Place from boutique hotel The Dominican show on the map that also attracts guests with its romantic and refined design. The rooms mostly feature trendy contemporary look and are decorated with luxurious paintings in the Renaissance style. The hotel has simply everything needed for a comfortable stay a stylish lounge with a rich choice of treats and a bar with a wide choice of exotic cocktails. Besides that, travellers are always welcome at the spa with sauna and massage rooms.

B&B Garden in the city, Gent
A hotel with a symbolic name, B&B Garden in the city show on the map also ideally suits travelers who seek peace and serenity. Light colored rooms made in exclusive style and decorated with flowers, paintings with miraculously beautiful landscapes on the walls, a silent inner yard with benches and tables this amazing hotel will be a perfect fit for couples of different ages. There are many beautiful and interesting places for walking near the hotel, as well as wonderful restaurants and shops.

Hotel Prinse, Antwerpen

Couples, who seek an elegant and a very romantic place to enjoy their intimate vacation, are recommended to take a look at Hotel Prinse show on the map. The building of the hotel was constructed yet in the 16th century and is located right in the heart of the historic district of Antwerp. The majority of the hotel's 30 guestrooms are intended for couples. All guestrooms have luxurious modern furniture made of wood and are decorated with designer fabrics in coffee shades. All guestrooms look very romantic because of a special lightning system with precise tuning that includes numerous miniature lamps. During warmer months of the year travellers are welcome to relax in a cozy inner yard with garden and terraces, and the hotel's bar is a wonderful place to taste delicious signature cocktails.

B&B Au Grenier, Gent

Despite its modest status, B&B Au Grenier show on the map never ceases to draw the attention of couples. The miniature hotel is located away from the noisy central part of the city and is surrounded by large fields and meadows. B&B Au Grenier occupies a beautiful historical mansion and offers only two guest rooms made in mostly light colors, as well as various extra services for guests in order to ensure they have a wonderful vacation. Guests of B&B Au Grenier can relax in the garden that has a large outdoor swimming pool and spacious terraces for sunbathing. Active travelers can rent bikes, make a picnic, or enjoy a walk in the picturesque surrounding nature.

B&B Koto, Antwerpen

Perfect for a secluded and private stay, B&B Koto show on the map is located in the historic district of Antwerp. The hotel offers only two luxurious guestrooms for couples. One absolutely fabulous room is located on the mansard. This guestroom has slanted ceiling and original beams, and there is a window right above the bed. A cozy inner yard with a seasonal swimming pool and sunny terraces is one more advantage of the hotel.

Brugsche Suites Luxury Guesthouse, Brugge

Brugsche Suites Luxury Guesthouse show on the map is a charming mansion that has only three stylish suites. The rooms feature all modern amenities including a spacious bathroom and a living room with a fireplace. Decorated with antique furniture, the suites have the charm and appeal of a rich house. The hospitable atmosphere and luxurious furnishing of this high-class guesthouse will please even most discerning travellers. Brugsche Suites Luxury Guesthouse will be a perfect choice for travellers who seek serene and calm pastime.

Monty Small Design Hotel, Brussels

Miniature and inexpensive Monty Small Design Hotel show on the map is located in a very beautiful old house. This hotel will draw the attention of travellers who are fond of non-standard designer ideas and designer approach. Red color, which dominates in the hotel's design, makes travellers more active, maintaining the atmosphere of love and passion. The hotel is proud of its informal style of service.

There is no restaurant at the hotel, so guests are invited to have breakfast and dinner at one big table installed in the lounge zone. During their stay at the hotel, travellers are welcome to use bicycles to explore the city or leisurely relax in the garden or on the terrace, away from city noise and stress.

Engelen aan de Waterkant, Gent

Travelers, who prefer classic style accommodation, will be fond of Engelen aan de Waterkant show on the map. Its spacious rooms are distinguished by large size and are made in crisp white and coffee shades. The presence of elements of décor in the style of past centuries, such as beautiful crystal chandeliers, elegant handmade wooden furniture, interesting marble figures, and white table lamps creates a special and refined atmosphere. Guests can relax in a peaceful atmosphere not only in their rooms but also in the charming inner yard that is decorated with exotic flowers and plants.

Yellow Submarine, Antwerpen

If an unhurried vacation in a romantic setting is what you crave for, pay attention to Yellow Submarine show on the map. This wonderful hotel is located in walking distance of the Grote Markt. The hotel has only three beautiful guestrooms, and all of them are intended for couples. The guestrooms are beautifully decorated with lightwood, with a giant crispy white bed occupying the central part. The hotel is located in a historic building, and much of the original décor has been carefully preserved till our days, making the hotel even more charming. Even bathrooms are very unusual there and have round bathtubs.

Maison Bousson, Brugge

Located in a peaceful area, Maison Bousson show on the map is a small boutique hotel with beautifully decorated elegant rooms, which are nothing but perfect for a romantic vacation. Various facilities, such as an outdoor swimming pool, will make your stay at Maison Bousson very comfortable. Active travellers are offered to make a bicycle ride in the hotel's garden. When it's cold outside, there's nothing better than to relax in a cozy hall near the fireplace. The atmosphere of calmness, peace and comfort will surround you during your stay at romantic Bruges.

Extraordinary hotels

Extraordinary accommodation in Belgium most original and unusual hotels

Sonntag in Lüttich Belgium is not the most popular country for tourism. However, there are wonderful hotels and motels here, some of which are unusual and unique. The hotel "Barkentijn Marjorie" in the port of Antwerp is a really big ship built in 1930, and you can take a cruise on it. In Kemzeke, tourists will find, perhaps, one of the strangest and most indecent hotels in the world called "CasAnus". And this is exactly what its name tells us, the rectum. "La Balade Des Gnomes" is a fabulous hotel in Heyd. It has the shape of a cow or horse, and each of the unique rooms transports guests into a world of fantasy.

Hotel Le Tissu, Antwerpen

Travellers, who want to spend several days in an unusual hotel with rich history, should pay attention to Hotel Le Tissu show on the map. This hotel is open in an old house that previously belonged to a priest. The old house was transformed into a five guestroom hotel, where every room features individual style and expensive decorations. All guestrooms have antique furniture and the guestroom on the mansard features the original wooden beams. The magnificent and intimate hotel is very popular with couples; during warmer months, guests are welcome to relax in a charming inner yard with terraces.

B&B Contrast, Brugge

you will find B&B Contrast show on the map hotel not far from Grand Place Square, surrounded by a beautiful garden. The hotel is open in a restored single-storey building and offers only 5 comfortable guestrooms. The hotel looks very catchy because of its architectural style it feels like the hotel makes a unified whole with the nature surrounding it. Many guestrooms come with a private wooden terrace; there is also an originally looking glass covered gallery at the hotel. The garden surrounding the hotel deserves the closest attention besides interesting landscape decorations, there is a rich collection of sculptures. Some guestrooms of this unusual hotel offer charming views of the canal.

Ghent River Hotel, Gent

The history of Ghent River Hotel show on the map is quite interesting. The hotel is open in the building of a former ancient factory near Botermarkt Square. Walls of the grandiose and elegant building hide an inimitably charming historic atmosphere. The building was restored extensively with the original wooden and stone décor fully preserved. Guest rooms are made in different styles there are retro style beds in some rooms, while in the others guests will find an ultra-modern design. The beautiful hall with arched floors is now used as a restaurant, and when the weather permits a part of the restaurant's tables are installed in the inner yard.

Hotel Rubenshof, Antwerpen

An absolutely unique place, Hotel Rubenshof show on the map is a kingdom of modern. The hotel is located in an outstanding historic building with original, carefully restored frescos. The beautiful frescos can be seen on the walls and ceiling of public zones. Some windows still feature original stained-glass panels and detailed carvings in the hall are gilded.

B&B Koetshuis, Brugge

B&B Koetshuis show on the map remains one of the most secluded and romantic hotels in whole Bruges. It has only two charming guestrooms open in a wing of an old mansion, which is hidden by a lush garden from prying eyes. The hotel is designed in accordance with traditions of the past, and so it will be a wonderful destination for a romantic vacation. Every day, guests of the hotel will be able to relax in the picturesque garden in the daytime, and in the evening they are welcome at the lounge bar that serves best Belgian beer. There are many interesting sights near the hotel, including the Church of Our Lady, Minnewater Park and an ancient castle.

Chalet De Maalte, Gent

Chalet De Maalte show on the map stands out of the list of other hotels. This wonderful hotel will impress nature lovers. Chalet De Maalte is open in Parkbos Park, the total area of which exceeds 14 hectares. The unique décor of guest rooms is in line with the surrounding splendor of nature. Giant panoramic windows with breathtaking views of the park, woven handmade furniture, cream shade fabric draping, and wallpapers with floral print guests are guaranteed to feel connection to nature. There are comfortable terraces and picnic areas near the hotel.

HotelO Sud, Antwerpen

HotelO Sud show on the map is located in a beautiful historic building with white walls. This hotel should be definitely present in the rating of the most unusual hotels of Antwerp. Unusual, one of a kind design developed by talented modern professionals has become a calling card of the hotel. Every guestroom in the hotel is unique and has its own peculiarities. For example, in some guestrooms walls, floor and ceiling are fully covered with wood. Even bathroom design is absolutely uncommon in this hotel bathtubs are completely made of wood. The hotel is famous not only thanks to its design, but also because of Nero Beer Restaurant. This stylish restaurant is loved by both locals and guests of the city.

Charlie Rockets Youth Hostel, Brugge

The choice of quality hostels and budget hotels is really wide in Bruges. Charlie Rockets Youth Hostel show on the map is often called the most unusual and creative hostel in the city. Located just several minutes away from the Market Square, this hostel features truly creative and colorful design. Charlie Rockets Youth Hostel is open in a historic building and some elements of design, such as fragments of the original wooden carcass, remind visitors that they stay at an antique place. The bar has become a calling card of the hostel. Made in the style of the middle of the 20th century, the bar serves signature cocktails and best sorts of Belgian beer.

Hotel BLOOM, Brussels

Often recognized as a landmark in Brussels, Hotel BLOOM show on the map is a large design hotel with more than 300 comfortable guestrooms. All guestrooms are made in different styles with white as the dominating color and interesting artistic patterns on the walls. The hotel's restaurant, Smoods, is another advantage of this magnificent place. Besides tables, the spacious hall of the restaurant has become the last resort to a retro Volkswagen minibus. By the way, one table is installed inside the bus. A dinner in such an unusual setting promises to be mesmerizing.

Monasterium PoortAckere, Gent

Monasterium PoortAckere show on the map is a one-of-a-kind place where travelers can stay in the building of an ancient Neo-Gothic monastery. Cells of the monastery have been transformed into comfortable rooms that are now decorated with premium hardwood floors. Some guest rooms have old wooden beams. In the morning, the magnificent dining hall of the hotel is used to serve breakfast, and in order to relax guests are recommended to walk or sit in the charming inner yard with landscaped compositions.

Tips for Family and Kids

Family holidays with children in Belgium attractions and entertainment

You will find it convenient to relax with the whole family in Belgium because the country offers a variety of leisure options for both adults and children. You should not restrict yourself to walks and shopping only. Water Parks, Amusement parks and Interactive museums will take your breath away and the imagination of children and adults alike. Incredible rides and interesting exhibits will make the journey many times more fun. Combining pleasant and useful activities, fun and learning, you can have a holiday that every family member would like to repeat. Therefore, you can safely take the little ones on the trip Belgium is waiting for guests of all ages with open arms and lots of pleasant surprises.

When choosing an amusement park, it is best to opt for "Walibi Belgium". It is located near Brussels and is one of the largest parks of its kind in the country. Guests will find more than three dozen rides here for adults and children. The young ones will enjoy the merry-go-rounds, dragon boat, riding a small train and much more. The park offers many adventures for the whole family, for example, walks along the river. In addition, there are extreme rides here too. You can grab a snack at one of several restaurants situated here, and the park proposes you visit its 4D cinema. "Aqualibi", an aqua park with a large collection of water slides, a pool with artificial waves, hot pools and a children's area, awaits lovers of swimming.

The amusement park "Bellewaerde" located near Ypres, offers ridiculously dramatic entertainment on a fast river, conquering heights on exciting rides, a swift descent from a water slide, trips on small cars and trains, and even a meeting with real tigers and lemurs. "Plopsaland De Panne" is located in De Panne. For almost twenty years of its existence, this park has become one of the favorite amusement spots of the Belgians. Shows are often held here, and you can reserve a place for festivities (for example, children's birthday parties), and the wonderful attractions rarely leave anyone feeling indifferent. What could be more exciting than playgrounds, roller coasters, chatting with horses?

"LAGO Lier De Waterperels" in Lier is more of a wonderful public swimming pool than a full-fledged water park. However, you can spend a few hours here without noticing how time flies by. Within the territory of the park, there are two outdoor pools, an indoor sports pool, a sauna, two children's pools, a "lagoon" with warm water and a water slide, a large water slide for lovers of extreme sports, a terrace and a cafe. One of the most popular parks in Belgium is called "Zilvermeer". It is located in the Mol and offers the opportunity not only to have fun in the water but also to spend the night in one of the cozy and comfortable guest houses on its territory. An excellent restaurant, plenty of space for walking and cycling, and a clean beach makes this place something more than just a water park.

It may seem difficult for tourists to pick out one from a variety of Belgian museums, especially those that will be suitable for children. Whatever your choice, there is one museum in Belgium that is definitely worth a visit. This is the Museum for Old Techniques in Grimbergen, which has been operating as an educational center for more than thirty years. Indeed, this place is more than just a museum. In addition to the permanent exhibitions devoted to woodwork, blacksmithing, and bread making, there is an attic for children from the ages of 3 to 12 years old. Here they are invited to participate in building and creating things by themselves. They can also play music and express themselves in other ways. The museum also has workshops for adults.

In Mechelen, tourists will find a wonderful Technopolis, ready to offer adults and children an incredible amount of activities. Sports, science, and technology are the main directions of this research center. Here you can build a house, learn a lot of new things about the human body and animals, work as a baker, discover the interesting properties of light, and see real robots.

Children and teenagers will definitely enjoy visiting the Euro Space Center in Redu. Here education goes hand in hand with entertainment. Adults and children will enjoy movies about space and technology, and interesting modern exhibits. Also in the center, there is a moonwalk simulator. It will be interesting to walk through the beautiful Castle of Bouillon, which took its name from the city of Bouillon, where it is located. This is a fortress of the Middle Ages, where you can stroll while enjoying the undisturbed atmosphere of the semi-dark rooms. Performances with birds of prey are held here, as well as guided tours with torches

Shopping

Shopping in Belgium outlets, shopping streets and boutiques

As in any other European country, there are many shops, markets, shopping centers and boutiques in Belgium. Guests of the country will easily get into a fuddle if they do not know what they want to buy and where to buy it. One of the most popular supermarkets in Brussels is "Woluwe Shopping Center". For half a century, it has been offering high-quality goods to its customers. This is a convenient shopping center in a prestigious area of the city. Famous brands such as "H & M", "Chanel" and "Zara", as well as less known prestigious and affordable Belgian brands, sports accessories, sushi, and great ice cream are all within your reach in "Woluwe". Exhibitions and art fairs are often held in the mall. The center is however closed on Sundays.

The "Waasland Shopping Center" in Sint-Niklaas sells mostly not the world's most well-known brands, but anyway they offer a huge amount of other brands. When customers want to eat something after an entire day of shopping and getting acquainted with interesting firms, they can choose from more than twenty options. There is a supermarket in the mall. Various events are also held here often, including those for children. The center is open from 10 am to 8 pm daily, with the exception of Sundays. Antwerp invites you to shop at "Shopping Stadsfeestzaal". This is a three-storey spacious mall with an additional basement floor and a large number of shops, stalls, and boutiques. You can spend an entire day here buying cosmetics, chocolate, muffins, accessories, clothes, underwear, shoes, household goods and products. The center is open from 10 am to 6:30 pm, except on Sunday.

The Maasmechelen Fair is named after the city in which it is located. This is an outlet center that has been operating for more than 25 years. Customers will find shops of brands such as "Swarovski", "Tommy Hilfiger", and many others in it. The fair is popular among tourists due to the excellent assortment of products and favorable offers for guests of the country. Therefore, it would be best for tourists to visit the fair during the summer holidays. The opening hour is from 10 am to 7 pm daily. Tongeren flea market is a great place to buy memorable souvenirs. This is one of the largest markets of its type in Belgium, stretching across several streets. Buyers will find here antique shops selling tableware, furniture, decorations, and other goods. The market is popular among tourists and is known for its fairly high prices. You will find it open on weekends.

The "Grote Markt" which opens on Wednesdays is a farmers market located in the center of Bruges. Here you will find cheeses and sausages of different types, sweets, flowers, and plants in pots, vegetables, and fruits. This place is worth visiting by every guest of the city, even those who are not going to buy anything. This is so because the place is so charming that it is nice to just walk around it, admiring the beauty of the buildings. There is a very old Sunday market called "Marché de la Batte" in Liege. It is located on the banks of the river and is usually quite crowded. Prices of goods here are mostly low, and the choice of fresh vegetables and fruits is wide. You can even buy puppies and kittens here. Clothing is sold on the market, but it is better not to go for them as they are of poor quality, but the bread here is however always fresh and tasty.

The antique market in the center of Tongeren sells mostly antique furniture and books. The market is quite large and is suitable not only for shopping but also for walking. It has been in existence since the 70s of the last century. You can find here products of the 19th century, as well as more modern vintage ones: statues, paintings, and candlesticks everything that can add elegance to any home. In Bruges, there is an interesting store called "'t Apostelientje". Things like wonderful antiques and real hand-made Bruges lace are sold here. The famous lace being sold in many places in Belgium is fake, therefore you should only visit this store ('t Apostelientje) if you intend to buy genuine lace. 't Apostelientje has been operating for about 30 years and have never disappointed customers. Paintings, furniture, books, are some of the real antique items.

The boutique brand "Moncler" is located in Antwerp. Here buyers will find a large selection of high-quality and stylish men's, women's and children's clothing. In "Moncler" clothes, you easily stand out from the crowd because of their unusual, but neat and attractive look. The store must be visited by lovers of everything unique and unusual. The store Madame Mim in Bruges sells hand-sewn unique dresses and original jewelry. Clothes are sewn by the shopkeeper, who is glad to receive every buyer.

In the mind of every guest of Belgium, towards the end of the trip, the question arises: what would one buy as a souvenir that will not rake up dust in the closet, but serve as a pleasant reminder of the trip? When it comes to edible souvenirs, you will want to treat those closest to you with, we must not fail to mention chocolate of various types from ordinary tiles and sets to lipsticks as well as excellent waffles and cheeses. It is better to buy all these items at specialized stores, where there is a wide range to pick from. Some goodies can, however, be found in ordinary supermarkets. In addition, you should pay attention to the clothes and accessories of the Belgian brands, which are always distinguished by originality. Real Belgian handmade lace should be bought only in boutiques to eliminate the possibility of acquiring a fake.

Tour Advice

Travel tips for Belgium what to prepare in advance and what to obey

1. Flemish and Walloons cannot be confused in any case. The Flemish live in the north of Belgium and speak Dutch, or rather, its dialects. The Walloons, on the other hand, inhabit the south, with their languages being French and Walloon. To confuse these groups or their

languages is going to be perceived as an insult by your Belgian interlocutors.

2. It should be firmly remembered which languages are spoken in certain parts of Belgium. Those who have decided to go round the whole country will have to learn basic phrases in English, Dutch and French. In the capital, you can speak English and French; in Flanders, it is best to communicate in Dutch, but residents will also understand English; in Wallonia however, tourists will have to switch to French as most of the locals do not speak English or Dutch.

3. Going across the pedestrian crosswalk when the traffic light is green, be sure to carefully look in both directions. There are a lot of reckless drivers pressing everyone's luck on the road, so taking extra caution will not only preserve your health but also your life.

4. Those invited to the Belgians usually bring a floral bouquet (but not chrysanthemums, these are mourning flowers), and there must be an odd number of them. However, 13 flowers are the worst idea this is an unlucky number and can spoil the mood of the receiver. You can bring a set of sweets, and save up a good wine for those Belgians with whom you have already established a friendship.

5. Belgium is one of the most tolerant countries in Europe. Its citizens believe in equal rights for all people. Therefore, even the slightest manifestations of sexism, racism, homophobia and other types of

intolerance for most Belgians will be a sign that the interlocutor is a barbarian and a dummy. You should not joke about these topics either. For this reason, guests of Belgium should keep track of their own words so as not to be driven out of decent society in disgrace.

6. Belgians love to complain. Bad weather, noisy public transport, stupid songs on the radio, expensive fruit almost anything can cause an emotional outburst. Therefore, it is possible and necessary to complain here, and it is likely that the tourist's indignation will be happily shared by his interlocutors.

7. When visiting Belgium, it is important not to forget to take along an umbrella or a raincoat. The country is known for frequent rains, and the clouds can come quite unexpectedly. Heavy showers are rare, but very few people will be pleased to be soaked in the rain during a walk.

8. For tourists who want to make friends in Belgium or just chat with strangers, it is better to go to any event or place that creates this opportunity, like a membership club or exhibitions. But trying to start up a conversation with strangers in a vehicle, elevator or store is not appropriate; the Belgians do not like it. Also, it is best not to approach strangers at all in public places here they respect personal space and expect the same from others.

9. Shopping in another country is always very interesting, only that in Belgium, it is better to avoid shopping on Sundays. Most of the stores

on this day of the week are simply closed, and the few that do open are always filled with lots of people.

10. You cannot pay someone a visit without being invited or notify your hosts about your arrival in just an hour. In Belgium, everything is always planned out, so the unexpected appearance of a guest can disrupt the plans of the Belgians. You should not invite your friends for a walk or an event at the last moment. Everything needs to be planned in advance; this can earn you the respect of the locals.

11. The Belgians consider being late even for informal meetings and events, as a sign of disrespect. You can be late for no more than five minutes. Otherwise, you will be tired of trying to prove to Belgian acquaintances that nothing offensive was meant.

12. It is better not to criticize the Belgians and not to make comments about them, and if this is absolutely necessary, then the remark should be presented in a gentle manner so as not to hurt their ego.

13. In Belgium, residents do not like people who are prone to boasting and laziness, as well as those who do not take good care of themselves and their homes. Guests of Belgium, who want to win the favor of the locals, should not give them a reason to suspect them of these shortcomings. The Belgians themselves are hardworking people who rarely brag about anything and are always sharply dressed, so their dislike for braggers, slackers, and dirty things quite justifies itself.

14. Littering the streets of Belgium is strictly prohibited. For the neat and tidy Belgians, this is one of the clearest manifestations of disrespect.

15. In Belgium, there are many clever and cunning fraudsters who are capable of cheating even the most cautious tourist in the twinkle of an eye. What is even worse is that some of them may contact the family of the unsuspecting foreign guest and complain on his behalf about serious problems and ask for money. Therefore, it will be reasonable to warn your loved ones about such a phenomenon in advance.

Belgium Major Cities and regions

Antwerpen

Sightseeing in Antwerpen

What to see. Complete travel guide

Antwerp is an amazingly beautiful city. Due to its cultural and historical places of interest, Antwerp has always occupied a special place among cities and towns of Benelux. The centre of Antwerp is home to numerous great museums and architectural sights. The Royal Museum of Fine Arts is known as the most famous museum of Antwerp. The Antwerp Cathedral is often called the most magnificent and fascinating building of the city. The majority of places of interest are located in the central part of the city, and so it's easy to visit all of them by simply walking from one sight to another. Therefore, there's nothing strange in the fact why Antwerp is so popular with tourists. More than that, if you get tired of walking, you can easily find a place for relaxation in one of numerous coffee terraces of Antwerp. Antwerp is attractive not only because of its historical places. The city's harbour is another sight that appeals to all kinds of travellers. Antwerp also plays the leading role in the sphere of diamond processing and sale.

> The Cathedral of Our Lady:. The spectacular tower of the Cathedral of Our Lady is also known as the highest cathedral tower in Benelux. It can be seen from many parts of the city. The tower is 123 meters tall and it is located right in the historical centre of the city. The first stone of this gothic cathedral was laid in the 14th century. However, it took two centuries to finish the work. The cathedral was built on the site of an ancient Romanesque church. Only in the 80s of the previous century, when archaeological excavations were started, the specialists could finally guess how the previous church looked like.

Unfortunately, almost nothing has remained from the original interior. In the 16th century, during the period of iconoclasm, the Calvinists destroyed windows, pictures, relics, burial-vaults and dozens of altars. Only some frescos and the image of Madonna, which was made of marble in the 15th century, have remained from the original decoration. The interior of the cathedral was created from the very beginning, and this fact makes the cathedral so special. Here visitors will see the decorations of absolutely different styles, such as Gothic, Baroque, Rococo, Renascence and Neo-gothic. The cathedral is also the location of 4 paintings by a world-famous artist Peter Paul Rubens. These are 2 diptychs (The Descent from the Cross, 1612, and The Erection of the Cross, 1609-1610), The Ascension of Virgin (1626) and The Resurrection of Christ (1612). Beautiful stained-glass windows, the pictures on which depict various biblical plots, look as fabulous as altars. The main altar features one more masterpiece The Death of Virgin by Abraham Matthyssens.

>The House of Rubens:. Without a doubt, Peter Paul Rubens is one of the most famous citizens of Antwerp. Travellers will find a lot of places that remind of the great artist throughout the city. Grundplats is one of the places where visitors will be able to see a monument dedicated to the master. His paintings can also be found in numerous cathedrals and museums of Antwerp. The House of Rubens, in which the painter worked and lived, has still managed to keep the atmosphere of Antwerp Baroque. Thanks to original furniture, pieces of art and works from the private collection of the master, guests will be able to feel the real atmosphere of the Rubens' times. Another great place to see a collection of paintings not only by Rubens, but also by Van Dyck and Matsys is the House of Rockoxhuis that has been perfectly restored.

> Grote Markt:. Grote Markt is a three-cornered square, which is considered the centre of Antwerp. When the weather is good, terraces

of cafes located at the square are always full of visitors. Grote Markt is surrounded by The Cathedral of Our Lady and the City Hall. The City Hall, which was built in 1561-1564, features the Renascence style with evident Flemish and Italian traces. The top part of the front side of the City Hall is built in the pure Flemish style, while niches and pilasters are the result of the Italian influence. Special attention should be devoted to the interior of the City Hall. Inside tourists will be truly delighted with the look of fabulous halls and huge frescos. Some halls are devoted to a particular theme. For instance, in the Hall of Weddings all walls are decorated with paintings dedicated to wedding ceremonies of different times.

> The Guilds houses:. Don't forget to visit the Guilds houses that are located in the northern side of the square. Unfortunately, these houses are not the original buildings. Most of the houses were burnt down in 1576, and later they were reconstructed. The biggest house is called the Spanish House (Pand van Spanje). You will find it at St. Joris Street 7. The façade of the building depicts a dragon and St. Joris, who manages to escape nearly inevitable death and kill the dangerous creature. The skilful artwork of the façade creates an illusion that the dragon may fall down at any moment.

The fountain, which is also located at the square, is decorated with the image of a Romanian soldier Salvius Brabo. The monument of the soldier is connected with a legend about the origin of the name

"Antwerp". Once upon a time a giant called Druon Antigoon lived on the bank of the Scheldt. He demanded an excessive fare from sailors, who sailed across the Scheldt. The sailors, who couldn't or didn't want to pay, had their hands cut off by the giant. Salvius Brabo called the giant, overpowered him and, as a symbol of his victory, cut off his hand and threw it into the river, just like Druon Antigoon did with other sailors. So, as the legend says, the name Antwerp goes from "handwerpen" "to throw a hand". Scientists also suppose that the name goes from the word "de aanwerp" "sandbank".

> Antwerp museums:. Antwerp is a real paradise for museum lovers. The Royal Museum of Fine Arts is the place where one can see not only thousands of works by old school masters (among which you can see, for example, pictures of Flemish primitives), but also approximately 1500 works by modern authors. By the way, this museum is the place that exhibits the biggest and the most beautiful collection of pictures by Rubens. The Museum of Modern Art (Museum van Hedendaagse Kunst Antwerpen MUHKA) mainly exhibits the works of Belgian artists of the 60s of the previous century.

The National Maritime Museum is situated in the oldest building of Antwerp het Steen. Amazing ship models and a section with real ships exhibited in the open air make this museum one of the most interesting places in the city

Antwerpen: Family Excursion with Children

Family trip to Antwerpen with children. Ideas on where to go with your child

There are many wonderful places for tourists with children in Antwerp, and the local zoo is definitely one of them. The beautiful zoo is located not far away from the railway station. Founded in the middle of the 19th century, the zoo has become home to more than 5,000 different animals. Besides spacious open cages, the zoo features many cozy zones for rest, charming cafes and special playgrounds for children. The historic zoo has even a planetarium, a greenhouse and a special house for penguins, so everyone will find something interesting to see in this magnificent place.

Travellers, who are keen on observing the underwater life, are recommended to visit the Aquatopia Aquarium that is located in a historic two-story building. Inside the building there are absolutely stunning large aquariums of different size and shapes, where visitors will see colorful exotic fish, sea horses, finger fish and even sharks. While in Aquatopia, don't forget to walk in the tunnel aquarium that never ceases to fascinate both children and adults. Interesting thematic events take place every week in Aquatopia, various educational programs for kids of different ages are also not rare there.

Pirateneiland Park is a very interesting place, a day in which will entertain all family members. Recently the park has got a new theme zone called "the Pirate Island". It was opened in a restored old warehouse. Children will be able to try various rides and attractions there, and pass through a series of challenges that would make them feel like true pirates of the Caribbean.

If you are in search of a good place for walking, simply head to Antwerp Miniature Park an amazing park full of precise miniature copies of the most famous landmarks of the city.

Fans of unusual and original entertainment will be satisfied with a visit to the Sint Anna Tunnel. A walk in the tunnel will be very entertaining for both adults and teenagers. This historic tunnel is made under the Schelde River. Participants of an excursion in the tunnel need to go down using a special ladder in order to enter Sint Anna. When you cross the river and reach the other bank, you will be rewarded with a breath-taking panorama of the city. This area is equipped with great playgrounds for children and in summer a beach is open there.

The art park known under the name Verbeke Foundation is another fantastic place for family rest. The park is located in Antwerp suburbs, in the village of Kemzeke. This is a marvelous and an unbelievably beautiful place with picturesque landscapes and intimate atmosphere that will be liked by both adults and children. It is easy to spend a whole day in the park. Verbeke Foundation was open in 2007; it occupies the area of 12 hectares. There are many beautiful trees in the park, and in summer the park is decorated with colorful flowerbeds.

However, spacious exhibition halls still remain the major attraction point of the park. In the halls, visitors will see a large collection of modern art.

When it comes to describing entertainment parks of Antwerp, Bobbejaanland should be mentioned first. This is not only a great theme park, but also a true historic landmark of the city. The park was open in 1961 and was founded by famous Belgian singer Bobbejaan Schoepen. Nowadays this is the largest theme park in Antwerp, where guests are able to try more than forty different rides. In Bobbejaanland visitors will find popular and thrilling rollercoasters, car rides and even a small aqua park with many interesting attractions.

Families, who love active rest and various sports events, will enjoy a visit to Antwerp Olympisch Stadium. The stadium was built yet in 1920, but it is actively used even nowadays. Football games are particularly frequent there as the stadium is the home arena of Beerschot football club. All football games always attract many fans to the stadium, making a visit to this wonderful stadium even more fun and entertaining.

Antwerpen: Unusual Weekend

How to spend top weekend in Antwerpen ideas on extraordinary attractions and sites

If during a vacation in Antwerp you want to stay away from noisy tourist sites, head to the bay. Not many travellers know about this picturesque place, so the bay area is not crowded, especially in the morning, when one can hardly see any passersby. Despite that, this place is very beautiful, the bay is surrounded with modern buildings, and white yachts look simply marvelous in urban landscape. There are comfortable benches near the waterfront, where one can sit and relax or enjoy breakfast in the open air.

The district of Sorenberg is one more attractive place that is not very popular with tourists. This district was founded yet in the beginning of the 20th century and it reminds of a fancy isolated town. Architectural landmarks in the art deco style remain the biggest attraction of this place. Local historic villas and guest houses are usually not mentioned in classic tour guides, as well as a miniature tramline that is known as one of the main attractions of Sorenberg. The line makes a circle around a giant flowerbed. This picturesque place is perfect for taking memorable photos.

If you want to purchase something original and make interesting and unusual gifts for your friends and family, head to Ace Lighting, a designer shop located on Kammenstraat . In this wonderful store everyone will find exclusive designer items. The owner of the shop is famous designer Tom Dixon. The items sold there are quite expensive, but that price is normal for exclusive designer items that can be hardly found anywhere else. Some people visit the shop simply as an art gallery because every chandelier or vase is a true piece of art.

Ladies, who want to purchase something exclusive for themselves, should visit Wooters Hendrix. This shop, which is located on Lange Gasthuisstraat, has been working for more than 30 years. It sells, probably, the most unusual jewelry in the city. Bird arms, skulls and other strange talismans that resemble ancient magic items are just a small part of the items sold there. Upon entering the shop, you will understand that it is hard to find anything similar in any other jewelry shop of Antwerp.

Fans of nighttime entertainment should not forget to visit Cafe danvers. This club was open in a restored church of the 16th century. As renovation works were very careful, the original style and atmosphere of the building were kept. Visitors of the club will be able to feel the atmosphere of a medieval basement. During many years the club has been chosen as a venue for performances of famous musicians and DJs.

If noisy parties are not your cup of tea, head to the River Dyle. This picturesque 86 kilometre long river crosses the historic part of Antwerp and its tremendously beautiful suburbs. A beautiful bank of the river is an awesome place for unhurried walks. Fans of longer walks and excursions are recommended to visit tiny towns located on the both banks of the river. The town of Wavre with its rich military history and the charming university town of Louvain with its original traditions are considered the most interesting places to visit in the area.

While exploring Antwerp suburbs, don't forget to visit Verbeke Foundation Park. It is located in Kemzeke village and it was open relatively not long ago, in 2007. This park will be liked by fans of walking in unusual places as it is decorated with fantastic artworks and collages.

Antwerpen: Cultural Sights

Culture of Antwerpen. Places to visit old town, temples, theaters, museums and palaces

The old castle named Gaasbeek is one of most striking sights of Antwerp. The castle was built in the 16th century. The first fortifying facility appeared on the territory of the modern castle back in the 12th century. However, it couldn't avoid the total destruction. Gaasbeek is one of the most significant historical landmarks of the country. Among the religious attractions of the city we can't fail to note is Saint Charles Borromeo Church built in the early 17th century. It is a beautiful architectural monument of the Middle Ages built in magnificent Baroque style. The walls of the church keep 39 works by Rubens. The pictures suffered greatly during the fire, but they were carefully restored.

You should definitely visit Plantin-Moretus Museum, the collection of which is devoted to the history of typography. The museum contains a large library, which stores copies of rare and old books. The halls of the museum are decorated with exquisite decor items, many of which have a long history of more than one hundred years. Museum of Diamonds is, without a doubt, no less interesting. The treasury of the museum stores priceless jewelry. Some of the masterpieces were created by goldsmiths in the 16th century. Koh-i-Noor the most beautiful diamond in the world is also stored here. Other local attractions that are worth visiting include Hoogstraat Street, which is the location of numerous historic buildings. You will also find here lots of interesting shops and souvenir outlets.

During an excursion to Maritime Museum visitors can learn much interesting about the development and establishment of the local port area. The location of the museum is also very interesting you will visit a beautiful Steen Castle, so this place of interest is attractive not only as a museum but also from an architectural point of view. The museum's collection consists of a number of interesting exhibits connected with sailing. You will also find here some beautiful models of ancient ships. Visitors can make photographs and step onto the decks of beautiful ships and explore their environment. Grote Markt Square is surely a great place for observing. Numerous beautiful historic buildings are located around it. This place is particularly attractive during the Christmas season as the square turns into a huge market.

You can feel the spirit of the old city by walking along the Vlaeykensgang Street this is a kind of hidden treasure of the world capital of diamonds; so to speak, a pearl among diamonds. The entrance to the street is covered by a high arch-door, and the street itself is situated far from the main square. The effort spent in finding it will definitely cause no regret. There are overhanging arches of old houses and fountains and all this creates an unforgettable atmosphere of immersion in the Middle Ages. On this street, artisans were at one time repairing and making shoes.

Middelheim Museum is a kind of open-air museum that attracts tourists from all over the world with its sculptural structures, which can be enjoyed for hours. The Building of Havenhuis on the other hand can be admired for eternity. This unusual architectural structure immediately draws attention. Just by looking at it, many are surprised by the architectural genius and mastery of the creator, and it is no accident to create such a masterpiece could only be the idea of a brilliant architect. And his name is Emiel van Averbeke. The building was constructed in 1922. Today, most of the interior rooms are occupied by departments of the Antwerp port.

Another remarkable feature of the city is that its territory is home to beautiful cathedrals. You should definitely not skip the "baroque gem in the Gothic garden" Sint-Pauluskerk however, you probably would not miss it, since the building immediately attracts attention with its incredible beauty. Upon entering inside, you can find the excellent altar of Rosencrantz, and nearby, the works of Rubens, Anthony van Dyck and Jacob Jordaens. Onze-Lieve-Vrouwekathedraal is another building that must be visited. It impresses with its grandeur, not to mention the fact that the visit itself will bring unforgettable impressions. Here you will sure get an aesthetic pleasure encountering the works of Rubens.

By the way, the life of this great artist is very tightly connected with the city. It was here that the painter carried out his creations. You will therefore find many of his works in the churches of the city. Definitely worthy of a visit is Rubenshuis, which houses a collection of paintings and sculptures of various artists. There is also a beautiful garden behind the house. A noteworthy landmark of the city is Pagaddertoren a watchtower, reminiscent of the Spanish dominion of Antwerp. The fact is that such towers were built in order to see when the Spanish ships sail for tribute. Information for fans of atmospheric species: the most beautiful sunset in the city can be seen from the port of Antwerp. From it is visible Havenhuis, some cozy streets of the city, and the beautiful waters of the river Scheldt.

Antwerpen: Attractions and Nightlife

City break in Antwerpen. Active leisure ideas for
Antwerpen attractions, recreation and nightlife

Antwerp is a perfect place for family holiday. Those tourists, who have come here with their families, should definitely visit the local zoo. It was founded over 150 years ago. Today the zoo is home to as many as four thousand animals. Tourists, who enjoy walking and shopping, will also find much interesting in the city. Widest choice of shopping centers, boutiques and restaurants can be found on Meir Street. You will be pleased and amazed by widest selection of jewelry stores. Sweet tooth travellers will surely find excellent chocolate in the best shops of the city Burie, Del Rey and Château Blanc. Don't forget to move your feet to Theaterplein Square on weekends this place turns into a large market on this time of week.

You will find best Belgian beer in Den Engel Pub; De Vagant bar is no less popular. However, these are not only great places for lovers of this amazing drink. We suggest visiting Kulminator bar, where guests can enjoy more than 700 types of beer, as well as most unusual and exotic snacks. There are surely many nightclubs in Antwerp. The most popular of them are Noxx, Red & Blue, Pure, Nanno sur l'O and Café d'Anvers. The majority of nightclubs, restaurants and bars are surely located in the central area of the city. Industria nightclub becomes a hot place on weekends as most colorful and joyful parties take place here. Entertainments, which are organized by the club for its visitors, cover a large choice of actions. Only here you can attend original theme parties or concerts of popular music groups. Black Pearl nightclub surely cannot be ignored too. The music here never stops until dawn; the club has become a permanent place of rest for lovers of dancing and disco. The absence of dress code will also please visitors. The doors of Black Pearl club are open to all visitors.

Middelheim Park is the best place for relaxation and walks. Another advantage is that this park is located near the city. You will also find a museum under the open sky on the territory of the park. The museum features a rich collection of sculptures.

The best way to explore Antwerp is by bike, especially when local people prefer eco-friendly means of transport. There are plenty of such services throughout the city, but we recommend to take a bike tour at the CYCLANT Bike Tours, which is located next to Antwerp Central Train Station. There you can rent the bike and enjoy the trip with your friends, or take the guide and choose one of the offered tours to your liking. The most popular tour is called Marnix that combines the excursion to the old city, and few interesting neighborhoods on the outskirts of the city. When biking, you will enjoy the variety of cycling lanes and St.Anna Tunnel, which takes pedestrians and bicyclists under the river Scheldt. If need some rest after cycling all over the city, the guide will make a break at one of the bars, where you can treat yourself with a Belgium beer.

If you got tired of the city and need some rest on nature the best choice is to visit the natural park called Grenspark de Zoom. On the entrance, you will find a cozy parking place. It is the best place to have fun at summer, have the picnic and play various summer games. On the territory, you will find snack stands with traditional Belgium food. Thinking about the romantic and amusing trip that will stand out in your mind? Our strong advice is to take the balloon flight. The feeling of freedom and satisfaction will capture your mind. Apply to Airventure Ballooning service and choose your specific tour across the Belgium. The flight will take from one hour and a half, and up to six hours and will cost you from €145 per person. The team, who really loves what they are doing, will take you and your friends to the remote outdoor range and bring you back to the launch site.

The variety of aquaparks will satisfy the fans of water rides and activities. There are five aquaparks in Antwerp, and all of them located in the range of 40 kilometers from the center. The most popular is the Aqualibi water park with tropical atmosphere; it opens at the beginning of April and is located at Boulevard de lEurope. Here your family and friends will enjoy the biggest jacuzzi in Belgium, water machine, and rivers

Antwerpen: Cuisine and Restaurant

Cuisine of Antwerpen for gourmets. Places for dinner best restaurants

Antwerp will amaze its guests by a large choice of gastronomy options. Fans of Italian cuisine should definitely visit the restaurant named Da Giovanni, which is distinguished not only by delicious menu and elegant interior. This is the place where you will always find nice music and staff ready to accept and entertain guests. Kommilfoo is also a popular restaurant dedicated to international cuisine. The special dishes of this dining facility include roast duck fillet and foie gras. The decoration of Pablos Tex Mex restaurant is reminiscent of the saloons from the movies about Wild West. Here guests will be served excellent delicacies, Mexican tacos and exotic cocktails. This restaurant has gained great popularity among gourmets from different countries.

If you visit this city during warm months, you should definitely visit Pottenbrug restaurant, which tables are located on the outdoor terrace. Here visitors will find popular dishes from Belgian and French cuisine. Italian restaurant Spaghettiworld offers to its visitors approximately twenty types of spaghetti. Besides the huge menu, the restaurant's moderate prices have made this place truly popular. The main visitors of this place are tourists and students. La Riva Restaurant is the most romantic place of the city. On evenings this place attracts couples of all ages. The menu contains dishes of Italian, Belgian and French cuisine.

If you want to explore the city's bars, move your feet to Tabac. The bartender of this place constantly offers new and original cocktails and snacks to visitors. Vacationers will be also pleased by the cultural program. Enjoying the delicacies of the local kitchen is much better while listening to modern music and watching spectacular dance performances. Romantic tourists will prefer De Vagant bar, which is always distinguished by its cozy family atmosphere. Here you will find more than two hundred types of beautiful Belgian gin, as well as several hundred varieties of liquor. In addition to exquisite drinks offered visitors are welcome to try original appetizers, salads and desserts.

In Antwerp, gourmets will easily find the most popular dishes of the classic Belgian cuisine, as well as many interesting regional specialties. Local national restaurants usually cook dishes from seasonal products, so menus tend to change several times a year. Asparagus is one of the most popular vegetables in the region, so local chefs use it in a number of dishes. Dozens of different soups, various vegetable ragouts, and garnish to various meat dishes the use of asparagus is, indeed, versatile.

Guests of Antwerp are welcome to try food with asparagus virtually everywhere, from small and inexpensive cafes to elite Michelin restaurants. Guests of Antwerp even have an opportunity to learn to cook asparagus in accordance with the national traditions if they decide to participate in interesting culinary master classes. As a rule, these master classes take place in the historic brewery of De Koninck.

Visitors can also sample the best varieties of local beer during excursions in the brewery.

In order to get acquainted with the most unusual gastronomic traditions of Antwerp, it is not important to visit expensive restaurants and spend large sums of money. All you need to do is to visit one of the local bakeries. The city is famous for its historical traditions of bread making. Local bakeries cook dozens of various types of bread, the recipes of many of which have been unchanged for centuries. Travelers wishing to learn how to cook the real Belgian bread by themselves are recommended to head to Bokrijk Museum. Several years ago, a bakery was opened in the territory of the museum, so now visitors can attend it and participate in regular master classes.

Steak remains the most popular local meat dish. Local chefs compare cooking a steak to art. RAS restaurant is one of the best places to enjoy the juicy meat. This restaurant is famous for cooking steaks in accordance with old recipes. French fries are usually the most popular garnish to the meat. Steak is also often served with a variety of sauces. Seafood dishes are widely present in menus of Antwerp restaurants. Numerous gourmets visit the city for the sole purpose of trying fresh mussels. This seafood is cooked in a variety of ways, and the so-called "sailor's mussels" is considered the simplest and the most frequently cooked dish.

It is safe to say that wafers are the most popular national dessert that one can find in virtually any dining venue in Antwerp. Local chefs have turned this simple, at a glance, dessert into a true culinary masterpiece. Fluffy Belgian wafers are served with whipped cream, fresh berries, and fruit, various syrups and chocolate. The dessert is inexpensive, and guests of the city can buy freshly baked wafers right on the street in numerous stalls. Tourists can follow locals and eat the dessert with a glass of cold beer by one of the local breweries

Antwerpen: Tradition and Lifestyle

Colors of Antwerpen traditions, festivals, mentality and lifestyle

The local people are very friendly to visitors and are always willing to talk to them about any topic other than politics. Tourists are not recommended to discuss national issues with the locals. The royal family is another taboo topic for conversation. In order to find answers to all other questions fell free to ask the indigenous people. They will always help you navigate the city and let you know how to reach certain attractions the best way possible. Antwerp is one of the world's most famous diamond cutting centers. The local people have learned this exquisite craft since medieval times. It is worth noting that modern masters keep working with gems according to an old technology, which is kept in secret. Diamond trade-fairs are surely one of the most important events in the life of the city. These fairs are held several times a year. They attract most famous jewelers from all over the world. Many visitors come to such fairs just like to museums this is the best place to admire the fabulous look of stones.

Many centuries ago local residents were famous as refined gourmets. They have remained very skillful in food until our days. The reason for this is in the fact that this large port city has always had a large choice of different types of food. Ships coming from distant lands brought delicious seafood, rare wines and liqueurs here, as well as unusual spices and seasonings a true dream of any chef or housekeeper. You can still see and taste this largest choice of food in Antwerp. Just visit one of the local restaurants and try it yourself. Each dining facility certainly offers original and exotic dishes made of finest ingredients.

The majority of tourists tend to get to Antwerp during Christmas holidays, which is always celebrated here with grand scale. If you visit the city during this period, you will find here interesting street performances, fairs, largest choice of dishes in restaurants, and overall festive mood. The cultural program will be especially liked by children, because they can participate in colorful presentations and funny games that are organized for them every day.

Antwerpen is the second largest city in Belgium, and it is worth noticing. Local people have an eye for entertainment; all the festivals and holidays draw the full house among local visitors and guests from abroad. Antwerpen's calendar of holidays is especially bright in summer when the majority festivals take place. Those who admire theater, cinema, music, and art should come here in July and August and enjoy one's time during the Zomer van Antwerpen the cultural, which gathers fans all over the Europe. The organizers of the festival collect the set of platforms under the open air; they can be found in parks, squares, public gardens and on the bank of the river Schelde.

What is the first association you have with Flandria? If beer and various beer festivals then you must see and enjoy the Bierpassie Weekend, the most popular beer festival in all Flandria. It attracts beer fans from all over the world. During the weekend up to 40 breweries present and treat the visitors with about 400 taps of beer. Later in October, another beer festival, called Modeste, takes place. This festival is dedicated to Modeste Van Den Bogaert the director of famous Antwerpen's brewery "De Koninck". During 50 years he was leading this beer factory, and only small and modest breweries participate in this festival.

Gourmands and gastronomic tourists must book tickets to Belgium, where the annual food festival Antwerpen Proeft takes place. Within this festival, professional chefs from all over the country cook the best traditional dishes and treat the visitors. The gastronomical satisfaction is guaranteed. Jazz lovers will enjoy the Jass Middelheim, the festival that usually brings joy to tourist in the middle of August. Earlier in July, all the city is waiting for a sailing regatta. About 650 thousand visitors are gathering at the Port of Antwerpen and greet 100 sailing ships, 400 navy officers, and cadets from all over the world. The sailing regatta leaves the port and stern to Portugal and Spain.

Antwerpen: Accommodations

Extraordinary hotels

Extraordinary hotels best choice for your unusual city break in Antwerpen

Carolus Boromeus Church, Antwerp Belgian fans of art Geert and Carla Verbeke-Lens opened a very unusual hotel that can hardly be found anywhere else in the world. Originally CasAnus was just a sculpture made by Dutch designer Joep van Lieshout. The sculpture is made in the shape of rectum and ends with anus. Nowadays, the sculpture is located in the park of sculptures in Antwerp. There is one guestroom in the rectum shaped home. The guestroom is heated and has shower and a bedroom. The cost of booking of such an original place is 120 euro per night. The price includes a breakfast and free entrance to the park. Despite quite a strange idea, many travelers decide to book the room of such a hotel.

Antwerp port is the location of a no less unusual hotel. Here travelers can stay at Sleeping Around, the hotel that is made of freight containers. Naturally, inner design of these container rooms is quite modest, but all necessary amenities including heating, bathroom and conditioning are present. Travellers, who want "extra comfort", can book one of the three containers with kitchen, dining room and sauna. The concept of "sleeping wherever you want" was the idea of Norwegian Geoffrey Stampaert. Using such an advantage of containers as mobility, the hotel makes a journey round the world, so it is possible to "take home to travel". Travellers, who are ready for adventures, are welcome to book one of the containers.

Hotel Matelote
From Antwerpen center 1.4 km

There is a unique boutique hotel near the Grand Place. Hotel Matelote show on the map is located in a restored building of the 16th century. Posh and elegant design of the hotel is one of its main peculiarities, and a skillful combination of historic elements and modern designer items make the hotel look very fresh and stylish. Guestrooms feature the original wooden carving and walls are decorated with large panels. Stunning crystal chandeliers are worth a separate mention. Finally, one of the most charming and romantic rooms in the hotel is located in the mansard. This guestroom will be a perfect choice for all couples.

HotelO Sud
From Antwerpen center 1.9 km

HotelO Sud show on the map is located in a beautiful historic building with white walls. This hotel should be definitely present in the rating of the most unusual hotels of Antwerp. Unusual, one of a kind design developed by talented modern professionals has become a calling card of the hotel. Every guestroom in the hotel is unique and has its own peculiarities. For example, in some guestrooms walls, floor and ceiling are fully covered with wood. Even bathroom design is absolutely uncommon in this hotel bathtubs are completely made of wood. The hotel is famous not only thanks to its design, but also because of Nero Beer Restaurant. This stylish restaurant is loved by both locals and guests of the city.

Hotel Rubenshof
From Antwerpen center 1.8 km
An absolutely unique place, Hotel Rubenshof show on the map is a kingdom of modern. The hotel is located in an outstanding historic building with original, carefully restored frescos. The beautiful frescos can be seen on the walls and ceiling of public zones. Some windows still feature original stained-glass panels and detailed carvings in the hall are gilded.

Hotel Le Tissu
From Antwerpen center 0.8 km
Travellers, who want to spend several days in an unusual hotel with rich history, should pay attention to Hotel Le Tissu show on the map. This hotel is open in an old house that previously belonged to a priest. The old house was transformed into a five guestroom hotel, where every room features individual style and expensive decorations. All guestrooms have antique furniture and the guestroom on the mansard features the original wooden beams. The magnificent and

intimate hotel is very popular with couples; during warmer months, guests are welcome to relax in a charming inner yard with terraces.

Stylish design-hotels

Stylish weekend in Antwerpen collection of top unique boutique hotels

De Witte Lelie

From Antwerpen center 0.9 km

The name of a small hotel De Witte Lelie can be literally translated as "White Lily". The hotel was founded by two sisters who wanted to make it the best accommodation in the luxury segment in Antwerp. Now we can say that they have succeeded in this. White is the main color in the design of the hotel: one can see it in white ceilings with beautiful fretwork, carved marble fireplaces, bright crystal chandeliers and white carpets throughout the building. There is also a charming terrace with a romantic garden and a fountain.

B&B Home@FEEK

From Antwerpen center 1.2 km

The concept of B&B Home@FEEK is "bed and breakfast". The hotel consists of three apartments that were designed in an original and unusual style by Frederik van Heereveld. He created a relaxing and luxurious look of the guestrooms that come with a tropical shower, hydro massage and a private separated terrace. Spacious multi-room guestrooms with modern furniture create the atmosphere of comfort, cleanness and freedom. They are perfect for a good relaxation.

Hotel Firean
From Antwerpen center 2.2 km

Hotel Firean is owned by the Iserbyt family. The hotel is often called the most charming hotel in whole Belgium and is well-known beyond the borders of the country. It is distinguished by its outstanding architectural style that is a wonderful combination of cozy classics and antiquity. Owners of the hotel do everything to maintain this special atmosphere and make sure guests are pleased.

Astrid Park Plaza
From Antwerpen center 0.4 km

Located in a building that is often referred to as a new symbol of Antwerp, Astrid Park Plaza was destined to become popular. The design was developed by American architect Michael Graves, who used modern trends while developing the look of the hotel. The result of his work is worth praise maximum of open space, interesting color combinations and stylish installations. As the territory of the hotel includes the unique Aquatopia Aquarium, the majority of guestrooms have a definite marine vibe in design. Shades of blue and green look fresh and attractive, and windows in the shape of portlights only add to the stylishness of this place. Due to its wonderful location, the hotel is a great place to see the majority of sights of old Antwerp by foot.

De Keyser Hotel
From Antwerpen center 0.2 km

One more wonderful hotel is located just a few steps away from the main railway station. De Keyser Hotel is located in a grandiose historic building. The outside look of the building is quite strict and modest, but inside guests will find charming atmosphere and modern design made mostly in beige shades. Floors in guestrooms come with lightwood parquet. Inside there are large white beds, black curtains and modern lightning with black lamp-shades. All guestrooms are decorated with beautiful paintings and a sophisticated conditioning system. Some guestrooms feature marble bathrooms.

Antwerp Hotel National
From Antwerpen center 1.2 km
Unique interior made in the style of the 60s of the previous century has become a signature element of Antwerp Hotel National. Black and red are the main colors in the hotel's design. All guestrooms are decorated with elegant wallpapers, exclusive tapestries and contemporary furniture. Original paintings, designer furniture and a built-in lightning system make guestrooms look really posh. The hotel's halls feature unusual art installations made of old vinyl records.

Hotel Banks
From Antwerpen center 1.2 km
Art hotel Hotel Banks has become very popular with travelers who are tired of standard same looking hotels. Located close to the Market Square, the hotel offers more than 60 spacious originally designed rooms. Couples will like romantic guestrooms designed in light colors and decorated with fabrics and faux fur. Some two-room guestrooms come with a bathroom with glass walls, and energetic visitors will like

bold colored rooms. Public spaces of the hotel feature wooden designer furniture and are decorated with interesting installations from pressed flowers and twigs.

Hotels with history

Preserved history of Antwerpen: long-standing and historical hotels

B&B JVR 108

From Antwerpen center 2.4 km

Antwerp is home to many historic hotels. Not far away from the central square you will find mini hotel B&B JVR 108 show on the map. The hotel, which is located in a wonderful historic building, has only three guestrooms. Owners of the hotel managed to keep old elements of the original design, such as a fireplace, wonderful antique furniture and old paintings in heavy frames. Besides cozy rooms, guests are welcome to relax in a beautiful small garden, and in the evening there is nothing better than to rest in a charming lounge near the fireplace.

B&B The Baron

From Antwerpen center 0.5 km

The luxury Baroque style town house, which was built in 1860, was transformed into B&B The Baron show on the map hotel. Its luxurious rooms made in retro style are simply stunning with their antique wallpapers, authentic historic furniture and precious artworks throughout the hotel. Guestrooms for couples are very charming and romantic as they have king size beds with valance, old paintings and finest china. Public zones are no less wonderful as the hotel's owners managed to keep the original décor, high ceiling with fretwork and carved columns.

Hilton Antwerp Old Town
From Antwerpen center 1 km
One of the most beautiful buildings in whole Antwerp has become home for Hilton Antwerp Old Town show on the map. This 200 guestroom hotel has elegant retro design in best traditions of luxury. Guestrooms are decorated with carpets, antique redwood furniture and bright tapestries. Besides outstanding inner design, the hotel is famous for its finest cuisine restaurant Brasserie Flo Antwerp, in which hotel guests will be able to try the best dishes of the national cuisine made from locally sourced seasonal products.

Hotel Rubens-Grote Markt
From Antwerpen center 1.2 km
One more renowned hotel, Hotel Rubens-Grote Markt show on the map, is also located in a magnificent historic building. Only several steps separate the hotel from the Cathedral of Our Lady. Only best antique items were used in decoration of the hotel's rooms, namely, antique furniture, old paintings and fabrics, and other precious carefully selected elements of décor. VIP travellers are recommended to pay attention to suites that come with a wonderful private terrace. One more secret of the hotel is hidden in its inner yard, where guests

will find a magnificent rest zone that is decorated with blooming flowers during warmer months.

Hotel Firean
From Antwerpen center 2.2 km
Hotel Firean show on the map is a family run small hotel that has become famous far beyond the borders of the city thanks to its one-of-a-kind historic design. The building of the hotel, which is a marvelous example of the art deco style, was built in 1929. The building belongs to the Iserbyt family, who decided to transform a posh mansion into a hotel in 1986. During more than 30 years the hotel has been providing the best service for its guests. The magnificent hotel has only 9 guestrooms decorated with precious antique items. All the rooms have different design, so a stay at this hotel will never be boring.

Hotel T Sandt
From Antwerpen center 1.4 km
Boutique hotel Hotel T Sandt show on the map is also very popular with travellers, who enjoy staying in historic places. Guestrooms of this unforgettable hotel have a very interesting concept of combining antique items with modern designer elements. Some guestrooms have the original wooden beams and windows. Public zones are decorated with marble, wooden ladders with carved banisters and old artworks. There is a wonderful bar at the hotel, where guests are treated with signature coffee and various cocktails.

Luxury accommodation

Top places to stay in Antwerpen most luxury and fashionable hotels

Radisson BLU Astrid Hotel, Antwerp

From Antwerpen center 0.4 km

Antwerp is rich in high class hotels. If you search for a luxury hotel in Antwerp, take a look at Radisson BLU Astrid Hotel, Antwerp show on the map. This magnificent hotel is located close to the central railway station and the zoo. The hotel shares the building with the aquarium. Travellers are welcome to choose from a wide array of luxurious guestrooms, suites and apartments made in exclusive designer style. As expected from a high class hotel, it provides various extra services for its guests, such as a wellness club with an exclusive in-door swimming pool. The hotel's restaurant offers a wide selection of popular national dishes and best types of Belgian beer.

Crowne Plaza Antwerpen

From Antwerpen center 3.1 km

A no less striking and prestigious place, Crowne Plaza Antwerpen show on the map is a great hotel that will leave even hard-to-please guests satisfied. One of the best wellness centres in the city, Octopus, is located in the hotel and all of its guests are welcome to use its marvelous swimming pool free of charge. On a paid basis, travelers can enjoy various types of sauna, massage rooms and a modern gym. In the evening, head to ANNA lounge bar, where guests are offered to try the most delicious dishes of Flemish cuisine.

Hyllit Hotel
From Antwerpen center 0.1 km
Many upscale guests of Antwerp choose to stay at Hyllit Hotel show on the map that is located in the heart of the Diamond Quarter. Guests of the hotel are welcome to book magnificent luxury rooms and suites with king size beds and exclusive tapestries. One of the best restaurants in the city, Gran Duca, is also located in the hotel and occupies its top floor and terrace. In this restaurant travelers can try best dishes of Italian and French cuisine, as well as wonderful wine. The hotel's spa offers a wide range of treatments, some of which are free for guests.

Ramada Plaza Antwerp
From Antwerpen center 2.6 km
Business travelers might prefer Ramada Plaza Antwerp show on the map as it is located right in the heart of the business district of the city. The hotel occupies a part of a modern skyscraper with panoramic windows. Elegant guestrooms are made mostly in caramel and coffee shades, and long term guests will be pleased with comfortable serviced apartments. Guests of the hotel can use sauna and gym every day free of charge. There is also a stylish night club in the building. Travellers, who prefer to spend their evenings in a more relaxed way, are welcome in Hugo's restaurant, which windows offer panoramic views of Hertogenpark.

The Plaza Hotel Antwerp

From Antwerpen center 1 km
A list of the best hotels of Antwerp would be incomplete without The Plaza Hotel Antwerp show on the map. Its luxury guestrooms are very charming and comfortable, and feature king size beds, elegant tapestries and classic design. Stylish Victoria bar remains one of the main attractions of the hotel. The beautiful bar is made in classic English style and has one of the largest collections of elite alcohol beverages in the city. The hotel's roof was transformed into a relaxation zone with panoramic terraces.

Van der Valk Hotel Antwerpen
From Antwerpen center 2.2 km
High class Van der Valk Hotel Antwerpen show on the map is located somewhat away from the city centre. The hotel has more than 200 spacious luxury guestrooms with designer furniture and large bathrooms. A large spa with sauna and a swimming pool, and a modern gym are just a few amenities present in this wonderful hotel. After a long day full of sightseeing and entertainment, there is nothing better than to enjoy delicious international cuisine dishes in the hotel's restaurant. In summer, the food is served both indoors and on a spacious open terrace

Romantic hotels

Antwerpen for couples in love best hotels for intimate escape, wedding or honeymoon

De Koning van Spanje

From Antwerpen center 1 km

De Koning van Spanje show on the map is a small, beautiful and very romantic hotel. This true gem with a wonderful private garden will leave many pleasant memories and you will want to return there again and again. Spacious guestrooms of the hotel feature luxury bathrooms with Jacuzzi. Breakfasts are served in the garden in a very romantic setting. Charming and intimate style of the hotel will be a perfect fit for tourists who seek privacy.

Charles Rogier XI is a small hotel that has only three romantic guestrooms. All the guestrooms were decorated by the owner herself. A fireplace with cozily snapping twigs can be found in the English style guestroom, a bed with valance and large mirrors in heavy frames are in the French style guestroom, and the Scottish style guestroom features shepherd's plaids and hunting trophies on the walls. The owner collected antique furniture for her hotel from different parts of Europe.

Yellow Submarine

From Antwerpen center 1.2 km

If an unhurried vacation in a romantic setting is what you crave for, pay attention to Yellow Submarine show on the map. This wonderful hotel is located in walking distance of the Grote Markt. The hotel has only three beautiful guestrooms, and all of them are intended for couples. The guestrooms are beautifully decorated with lightwood, with a giant crispy white bed occupying the central part. The hotel is located in a historic building, and much of the original décor has been carefully preserved till our days, making the hotel even more charming. Even bathrooms are very unusual there and have round bathtubs.

B&B Koto
From Antwerpen center 1.7 km
Perfect for a secluded and private stay, B&B Koto show on the map is located in the historic district of Antwerp. The hotel offers only two luxurious guestrooms for couples. One absolutely fabulous room is located on the mansard. This guestroom has slanted ceiling and original beams, and there is a window right above the bed. A cozy inner yard with a seasonal swimming pool and sunny terraces is one more advantage of the hotel.

Hotel Prinse
From Antwerpen center 0.7 km
Couples, who seek an elegant and a very romantic place to enjoy their intimate vacation, are recommended to take a look at Hotel Prinse show on the map. The building of the hotel was constructed yet in the 16th century and is located right in the heart of the historic district of Antwerp. The majority of the hotel's 30 guestrooms are intended for couples. All guestrooms have luxurious modern furniture made of wood and are decorated with designer fabrics in coffee shades. All guestrooms look very romantic because of a special lightning system

with precise tuning that includes numerous miniature lamps. During warmer months of the year travellers are welcome to relax in a cozy inner yard with garden and terraces, and the hotel's bar is a wonderful place to taste delicious signature cocktails.

Hotel Julien

From Antwerpen center 1 km

A complex of the 16th century buildings located around a charming inner yard is now known as Hotel Julien show on the map. This amazingly romantic place features charming guestrooms for couples. Guests can book a mansard room or a guestroom with a spacious bathroom that has a big window. This hotel has a state of art spa that was made in the restored 16th century basement. Here hotel guests can enjoy sauna, vapour bath and a relaxation zone with rain shower. The lounge bar is the best place for rest and entertainment in the evening, and in summer hotel guests can dine in the inner open air yard. This hotel will also be liked by active travellers as it is located close to Meir, the main shopping street in Antwerp, and other popular landmarks

Antwerpen: Shopping

Shopping in Antwerpen authentic goods, best outlets, malls and boutiques

Shopping in Antwerp can be an unforgettable adventure. Popular shops and shopping centers are located very close to outstanding historical monuments, so a shopping trip always resembles an exciting excursion. Meir Street is especially popular with shopping enthusiasts. It is a series of beautiful buildings of 18 19 centuries. Nowadays, high-end fashion boutiques and designer shops where you can buy exquisite things are located here. You can still find several cosy restaurants and cafes on this little street. This historical district is perfectly equipped for the great outdoors.

Chic diamond jewelery, which can easily be distinguished from other jewelries by the label 'Antwerp's Most Brilliant' has been remaining Antwerp's visiting card for many years. In search of the most luxurious jewelry you should go to the Diamond District, which is close to the central railway station. Here, are the most popular jewelry stores and workshops, in which artistic jewellery is offered at the most attractive prices. If the desired decoration is not found, then it can always be ordered. The connoisseurs of elite jewelry will be pleased to find out that many celebrities buy jewelry in the Diamond District of Antwerp.

Those who are desperate for something new, should go to the trendy Zuid District. It is also located in the historic area, so many popular stores are in historical buildings. It is here that famous designer boutiques are concentrated, including Ann Demeulemeeste store. This designer boutique is attractive because of year-round discounts. Dandies have always an opportunity to purchase one of the designer items with up to 60% discount.

Those who are not accustomed to spending enormous amounts of money to new clothes and accessories, will be interested in strolling around the Wilde Zee area. There are many shops and reasonable prices, where you can buy clothes of renowned brands. One of the largest and most popular is Antwerp's Verso store. Clothes and accessories brands D&G, Cavalli, DKNY, RL, Valentino and Versace can be purchased at the most affordable prices. One of the most attractive regarding prices is the Differente clothing store, located on De Keyserlei 50. Lower prices for stylish clothing in the city are really difficult to find. Here, for as little as 5-10 euros you can buy original T-shirts and shirts. Excellent children's clothing can also be found here. Despite low prices, the quality of clothing presented in the store always remains at a high level.

Travellers who prefer walking along colourful markets should definitely visit the Antwerp's Latin Quarter. Here, both Oriental market and Birds market run on Saturdays. There's everything here, from unique antiques and works of art, to real oriental sweets and spices. The birds market is considered one of the best antiquarian markets in the city. It is visited by collectors around the world. Such an amount of elegant antique dishes, vinous jewelry and works of art can be seen not in all antiquarian markets. Another attractive feature of the bazaar is that some antiques can be bought here at very low prices for 1 or 2 euros only. This antiquarian market of Antwerp remains a favourite tourist destination.

Brugge

Sightseeing in Brugge

What to see. Complete travel guide

Bruges is located in the Belgium province of West-Flanders that is approximately 2 hours away from Utrecht (Holland). In the 9th century this town was conquered by the Vikings, that's why the name of the city is likely to come from the Scandinavian word 'bryggia' that means 'port'. Bruges is situated not far from the North Sea, so it has become quite an important international trade centre. Later, in the Middle Ages, a big wall was built around Bruges.

> Beguinage. This is one of the main places of interest in Bruges. It was founded in the 13th century, though the majority of white houses appeared only in the 17th and 18th centuries. The arch bridge, which forms the entrance to the palace, was built in 1570. Beguine sisterhood doesn't live there anymore, and this place now belongs to the Benedictines from De Wijngaard convent. The house under the first number serves as a museum, so everyone can get an idea of Beguine's way of life. The kitchen, the dining-room and bedrooms are furnished in the style of the 17th century. Initially, the main chapel was made of wood, but, unfortunately, it burnt down. In 1605 a new

chapel in the baroque style was built on its site. Fortunately, it has remained undamaged till our times. Nowadays, everyone is welcome to visit the chapel. The chapel is famous for the oldest image of Our Lady in Bruges. The image was created in 1240. There is also an altar with the alabaster sculpture of Christ of the 17th century on the right.

Beguinage is situated near Minnewater Lake, which used to be a part of the canal that connected Bruges and Ghent. Nowadays it's just a small picturesque lake with beautiful swans swimming in it. There is an interesting legend in Bruges, which is connected with swans. When Maximilian of Austria raised the taxes again, Bruges citizens rebelled and captivated the city. They also beheaded the former town head, whose name was Pieter Lanchals (it means 'long neck'). When Maximilian got the power back, he made an order, according to which swans (because they also have long necks) are to be bred till the end of the world in Bruges. Do you know how to differ a female swan from a male swan? You can guess by the mark male swans have it on the right clutch and female swans have it on the left one.

> The chapel of the Holy Blood. The chapel of the Holy Blood was built on the site of Basilius Chapel of the 12th century. The beautiful church is a wonderful example of the Romanesque style. Visitors will see a colored wooden image of the Virgin with the baby (approximately 1300) on the right nave. Initially, the chapel of the Holy Blood was built in the Romanesque style, but in the 15th century after the

reconstruction it turned into a Gothic chapel. During the French revolution the basilica was ruined, and then it was rebuilt from the very beginning. Entering the church is free, but you will have to pay in order to visit the Museum of the Holy Blood. As the legend says, in 1150 a part of linen with blood of Jesus was brought from Jerusalem. The duke that had brought it ordered to build Basilius Chapel, where the relic was to be kept. We can't say for sure whether it's truth of not. Scientists have a theory that most likely the legend tells about Duke Baldwin IX, who brought it from the crusade to Constantinople in 1203.

The blood of Jesus is kept in an incredibly beautiful casket of 1817. Jan Crabbe, the master who created the casket, used approximately 30 kg of gold and silver, and more than a hundred of jewels. Every year on Ascension Day a solemn ceremony takes place in Bruges. The procession carries the casket through the streets of the city. The museum located nearby is a great place to learn the detailed history of the relic and the basilica. One can also look at the silver crown of the 15th century, which was presented by Maria of Burgundy, and some other interesting paintings.

> Grote Market. The central square of the city is located in the very heart of Bruges. At the square you'll find a lot of marvellous historical buildings. The Belfort built in the 12th century is one of them. The tower of this building is 83 meter high and it deflects to the left for a

meter. Grote Market is also home to various cafes and restaurants. By the way, carriage excursions also start there. This is a very popular kind of entertainment in Bruges.

Halve Maan. Halve Maan is a brewery, where the sort of beer called Brugse Zot (you can taste it in Bruges only) is produced. Long time ago the brewery also produced another sort of beer Straffe Hendrik. However, nowadays this beer is not produced anymore. Since 1564 this brewery has been located in the same building at Walplein Square, in the historical center of Bruges. Nowadays, the excursions to the brewery have become very popular. Of course, beer degustation is the culmination of every excursion.

> The City Hall. The fabulous City Hall was built by order of Jan Rugirs. It was finished in 1421. The front side of the building is beautifully decorated with small towers. Wall paintings are especially interesting. The City Hall is situated at de Burg Square.

Family and Kids

Family trip to Brugge with children. Ideas on where to go with your child

Simply no family vacation in Bruges can happen without visiting confectioneries and cafes, walking in picturesque parks and attending interesting museums. This wonderful city will certainly please sweet tooth travelers, who will be able to enjoy magnificent Belgian chocolate and various chocolate desserts simply everywhere. Do you want to pamper your kids with some premium sweets? If so, head to DUMON Chocolatier as this confectionery is considered one of the best in the city. Here visitors are welcome to choose from hundreds of types of chocolates, cakes, and cookies. Moreover, visitors can order chocolates or a cake in accordance with individual design and preferences.

A visit to the Chocolate Museum (Choco Story) will be a wonderful continuation of your exploration of delicious Belgian chocolate. The museum is located in one of the most beautiful historic buildings of the city. Visitors to the museum will learn how cocoa beans are grown and how chocolate is cooked. Choco Story exhibits an interesting collection of items, all of which, as it's not hard to guess, are made of chocolate. Moreover, the museum regularly hosts various interesting master classes for children, during which kids will learn to cook sweets by themselves.

Travellers, who prefer more active pastime, may prefer a visit to Boudewijn Seapark. This amusement park is located in the southern part of Bruges. Inside, visitors will find various water slides, a beautiful swimming pool, and special playgrounds for children. The park is proud of its dolphinarium, so spectacular shows with dolphins and seals as main performers take place nearly every day at the park.

If you're tired of walking and want to diversify your vacation with calmer activities, it's time to make a boat ride on Bruges canals. Children will be particularly fond of boat excursions as they will be able not only to make a refreshing and entertaining ride, but also feed birds that live there ducks and swans.

There are many toy shops and other stores that will be liked by children in Bruges. Kathe Wohlfahrt, which sells Christmas ornaments, is one of the most unusual shops in the city. It works all year round. Christmas celebrations are the most liked time of the year in Bruges, so the choice of decorations is truly amazing. Here visitors can buy exclusive ornaments and toys made of wood and glass. Everything at the shop is handmade, so every decoration is unique.

Nearly all children adore potato fries, and in Bruges they have an amazing opportunity to visit a museum dedicated to their favorite food. Frietmuseum offers a rich collection of items with interesting historic artifacts. Guests of the museum will learn that for the first time potatoes were brought to Europe from Peru and will see interesting devices that were used to peel and slice potatoes hundreds of years ago. There is a charming café on the ground floor of the building, which signature dish is not hard to guess.

When it's hot outside, there is nothing better than relaxing in serene atmosphere, making a bicycle ride with kids on shadowy valleys and then having a picnic in a picturesque place. All these and more you will find in Astrid Park. It is located in the heart of the city not far from popular tourist routes, but at the same time this park is distinguished by calm and peaceful atmosphere. It is possible to spend hours walking on picturesque roads, admiring the look of giant trees or feeding swans. There are wonderful athletic fields and playgrounds for children in the park.

Unusual Weekend

How to spend top weekend in Brugge ideas on extraordinary attractions and sites

Miniature Bruges is famous for its unique historic buildings, but observation of architecture landmarks is not the only possible pastime. Actually, there are many ways for travellers to enjoy a non-standard vacation in the city. There are some interesting places and entertainments that are not well-known to the majority of travellers, so you have a chance to enjoy an unforgettable vacation in Bruges and make your friends jealous afterwards.

Guests of Bruges have an opportunity to make a true act of tourist bravery and go up to the top of the guardian tower and look at the city from a height of 107 meters. Travellers, who want to reach such an amazing observation deck, should be prepared to go up a very steep ladder with as many as 366 steps. However, the reward a breath-taking view of the city is worth the effort.

If steep climbs are not your cup of tea and you prefer unhurried walks instead, it will be fun to find the narrowest street in the city! The street has quite an unusual name Blinde Ezelstraat or the street of a blind donkey. It is better to come to this area in the morning as closer to noon it's always crowded with tourists and it's getting quite complicated to walk on this street, leave alone making interesting photographs.

One more way to have an exciting morning is to make a boat ride on canals. This romantic activity will be liked not only by romantic couples, but also by people who are fond of historic buildings. It is possible to see some historic and architectural landmarks of Bruges in their full splendor only from the waterside. Morning is the best time for such a boat ride as streets are not yet full of other travellers.

Rides on canals of the city are quite a popular and sought after activity, but not everyone knows that it's possible to explore old streets and landmarks in horse carts. Beautiful carts with well-groomed horses can be seen in many central squares of Bruges, including Grote Markt, and travellers are welcome to rent them. As this is quite an expensive entertainment, experienced travellers recommend making such a ride with three or four other people in order to save.

If during your visit to Belgium you want to attend one of old breweries, head to De Halve maan. This brewery was opened yet in

1546, and it's famous not only for rich history and magnificent beer, but also for interesting excursions that regularly take place there. During such a tour, visitors will learn how the beer is made and sample best sorts of the popular drink. In the end, visitors will be guided to the observation deck on the roof of the ancient brewery in order to admire the charming views of Bruges.

If romantic vacation was the primary purpose of visiting Bruges, don't forget to visit Lake Minnevater also known as the Lake of Love. This is a true piece of serenity and calmness, and it's simple to spend hours relaxing and admiring the surrounding nature. The lake is also famous for a large number of birds that live there. It's even possible to hand feed majestic swans.

Chocolate and beer mugs remain the most popular souvenirs from Bruges. Travellers, who want to bring a more unusual gift, are recommended to visit the teapot shop. This shop is located near the central square on the street that leads to the old town. The unusual shop sells one-of-a-kind teapots that can hardly be seen anywhere else, for example, teapots that look like a car or a toilet bowl. Besides that, you will find rare types of tea and delicious Belgian chocolate there.

Cultural Sights

Culture of Brugge. Places to visit old town, temples, theaters, museums and palaces

Thanks to quivering and respect of citizens, Bruges is home to numerous architectural and historical monuments. The old castle of Counts of Flanders is located not far away from Bourg. The castle was built in the 9th century. A walk through the beautiful square will help to see the greatness of historical sites and learn many interesting facts about the city.

There are also natural attractions in Bruges. Minnewater Lake is one of them. It is considered the most romantic place in the city, and so many interesting superstitions and legends are connected with it. On evenings you can see many romantic couples on the lake who come here to admire the sunset and enjoy the intimate atmosphere. Among the major attractions of the city is also the bell tower of Church of Notre-Dame, which height estimates 122 meters. The bell tower is made in the Gothic style. This is also the second tallest building of the country.

Christ the Savior Cathedral is another bright religious landmark. It was founded in the middle of the 7th century. It is natural that nothing has remained from the original building. During the centuries of its history the church has survived in four fires, and has suffered greatly during the French Revolution. The cathedral, which travelers can see today, was built in the end of the 15th century. Talking about religious things, we simple can't fail to ignore and the Jerusalem church. The building of the church was completed in 1470. Experts in ancient architecture often compare it with its famous Church of the Holy Sepulcher. Fine stained glass windows are the main decoration of the cathedral. They were made in the early 15th century. The hall of the church is also the tomb of its founder Anselm Adorno. This church is one of the few religious monuments, which has never been subjected to strong restructuring during its centuries-long history.

Art lovers should not forget to visit Groeninge museum, which exhibits a rich collection of paintings. Among the cultural institutions of the city there are also some highly original ones, such as Museum of French Fried Potato, Chocolate Museum and Museum of Diamonds.

Torture Museum Oude Steen is an equally remarkable place where you can look at how inventive people can be here is a huge collection of torture materials. The faint-hearted and children are better off not going to this institution, but they are welcome to visit all other places. The Bruges Beer Experience is sure to capture everyone's interest, where, in addition to learning everything about the history of beer, you can taste a drink and choose the best variety for yourself, as a bonus. Among other museums we would note Sint-Janshospitaal, which is one of the first hospitals in the whole of Europe. In addition, the hospital is a wonderful example of medieval architecture.

It is difficult to imagine a more wonderful and enchanting place in Bruges than Ezelpoort. It seems like not just any gate, but a gate to a real paradise for lovers of history for sure. The attraction encompasses a lake which is home to swans of heavenly beauty, considered to be a kind of "paradise for animals" in Eden. Beguinage is another place where the tender soul of history aficinados will find true pleasure. However, everyone shoud go for a walk here as this is yet another peaceful place with swans swimming in the lake. Also, those wishing to experience an incomparable pacification are advised to visit Sint-Janshuismolen.

You can go for a nice walk on The Markt, a chic area where at every step you will meet an interesting building. You can also visit the Huidenvettersplein, where in addition to the cultural experience you will be visiting local restaurants and cafes, each of which is remarkable for its matchless interesting interior. In other words, it is in fact a continuation of cultural enrichment. Near the Market Square you can find the Provinciaal Hof one of the symbols of Bruges, the gem of Gothic architecture.

There are two buildings in the city; simply put, failure to visit them would almost be considered sacrilegious, if not downright cruel. Firstly, is the bell tower Belfort, rising to the top of which you can see the incredibly beautiful city of Bruges open up. If you visit this place in the evening, then there will be no limit to the pleasure you will get.

The second place is the Tower of Poertoren, an excellent example of the Romanesque style of architecture. Film lovers will recognize the footage from the film "In Bruges" although there are plenty of such places that could be recognized thanks to the film.

Fans of mysterious and mystical things will be delighted by visiting two places in the city: first, the Site Oud Sint-Jan (located next to Sint-Janshospitaal), where you can look at the tools of medieval medicine, imbued with the atmosphere of that period. Visitors are demonstrated dreadful scenes of the then conducted surgery. In addition, there is a collection of Hans Memling's paintings, which brings conflicting feelings. Another place Rozenhoedkaai is the embankment, on which you can make an unforgettable romantic walk. Something mystical emits from this place.

Attractions and Nightlife

City break in Brugge. Active leisure ideas for Brugge attractions, recreation and nightlife
Boating on the canals of the city remains one of the most favorite pastimes for both visitors and locals. During such ride you will be able not only enjoy the beautiful scenery, but also learn about the history of the city. Cycling is a no less attractive option for wonderful pastime. You will find large number of bike rental offices in Bruges. As a rule, they are located near popular hotels of the city. Fans of more unusual entertainments are advised to make a ride around the city on a horse-

drawn carriage. A walk along stone streets and elegant squares will be a real journey into the past.

Bruges will be surely liked by nightlife lovers and people who enjoy entertainments. B-in is considered one of the most popular nightclubs of the city. It is located on Mariastraat Street. A cozy bar with the same name is located next to the night club. It offers to visitors a huge selection of exotic cocktails, beer and branded snacks. The Cactus club will definitely attract lovers of various musical styles. On evenings, numerous dancing enthusiasts move their feet to the club. Several times a week experienced dancers organize here different classes for beginners. Finally, if you are tired of loud music and want some rest, a cozy bar is at your service.

During your walk in the shops make sure you don't forget to buy traditional souvenirs fine lace and chocolate. Steenstraat, Mariastraat and Simon Stevinplein are best places for shopping. Here visitors will find widest choice of boutiques and shopping pavilions. "Rococo" is considered the best lace store of the city, so no female will be able to leave this place without buying a memorable gift. «The Chocolate Line» is the best place to go if your aim is best chocolate. At a glance it may resemble a boutique or a jewelry shop sweets are laid out on beautiful display cases with lighting. The air in «The Chocolate Line» is soaked in the enchanting aroma of chocolate, which captivates from the first minute. Another popular "souvenir" that travelers love to buy is, without a doubt, cheese. In a shopping pavilion named «Diksmuids Boterhuis» you will find more than three hundred varieties of cheese that is produced in local factories. There is also a real gourmet cheese, imported from Switzerland, France and England.

In a tiny city of Bruges, there are many interesting ways to spend time with pleasure. If you consider yourself an active traveller, then the variety of entertainments will brighten your day and leave joyful emotions. For example, amazing opportunity to explore the city and see it from with a bird's eye view is to make the most real tourist feat to rise on top of a watchtower. Here you will be astonished by the look at the city from the height of 107 meters. Those who are not scared of height and really have the desire to visit this amazing observation deck should take into consideration that you will need to walk upstairs which contains 366 abrupt steps. The award for this heavy walk is worth it a smart view of the city.

If you would rather have a smooth walk along the streets than abrupt rise up then you must discover the narrowest street in whole Bruges. This street has the strangest name you have ever heard Blinde Ezelstraat, in English it means The Street of Blind Donkey. Just because of its name you must check it! The best time to see it is during morning hours. The reason is simple, during the morning the street is empty and you can make a lot of great photos. The most exciting and unforgettable way to discover the small city of Bruges is to take the flight on the balloon. Bruges Ballooning service provides these astonishing adventures that will not leave you with a bunch of emotions. The price of the tour is about 180 euros. You can choose and book the tour independently by visiting the official website or join some tourist companies.

If you are a great fan of an active recreation than you should pay attention to Boudewijn Seapark amusement park. It is located in several kilometres from Bruges and is the only park in the country which includes a dolphinarium. Boudewijn Seapark works from April to October, the dolphinarium works all the year round. It is possible to visit it even in the winter. The visiting hours are the following: from 10 till 18-00. The cost of tickets varies from 9 to 23 euros, depending on the age of the visitor. The most notable attraction you can find in the park is the Springride. This attraction allows children, whose height is above one meter. Here you will be able to feel a free fall from the height of seven meters. For children, the so-called Bobo attraction will be especially interesting. In fact, it is more than ten attractions under the same roof placed on the area of 2500 square meters.

Cuisine and Restaurant

Cuisine of Brugge for gourmets. Places for dinner best restaurants
You can find cozy pubs and restaurants almost on every street of the city. Speaking of pricing policy in the gastronomic facilities of this

place, it is worth noting that all most prestigious and expensive restaurants are located near Burg and Markt Squares. Tourists and students traditionally choose local kiosks called "fricatens", where you can buy everyone's favorite French fried potato and other snacks. The majority of the prestigious restaurants open after 6 pm. Among the fashionable restaurants of the city we surely should mention De Drie Zintuigen, which serves gourmet delicacies and rarest wines. Bruges is a true paradise for fans of drinking, because simply every bar and pub in Bruges features dozens of types of Belgian beer.

Thus, De Garre pub offers visitors to choose from as much as one hundred types of beer. It has its own brewery, which produces an exclusive brand of beer called Triple de Garre. Brugs Beertje pub is famous for its everlasting funny and relaxed atmosphere. In addition to beer you will always find here excellent meals. Perhaps, Vlissinghe tavern is the oldest institution of this kind in Bruges. It was opened in 1515. Here guests will be offered to try national cuisine in its classic version. Of course, there are more exotic facilities in Bruges. Narai Thai restaurant is one of them. Thai delicacies form the basis of its menu and, the restaurant's chef never ceases to amaze visitors with original author's masterpieces and a masterful combination of oriental spices.

Huidevettershuis restaurant is located right in the center of the city. The specialties of this place are traditional Flemish soup, roasted rabbit and home-made ham. In addition to widest choice meat delicacies, visitors are welcome to try vegetarian dishes, as well as excellent pickled herring. The opening of De Karmeliet restaurant was held in 1996. Since that time it has been considered one of the best restaurants devoted to the Flemish cuisine in the city. Here you can order fine fish soup with shrimps and numerous vegetable salads, and, of course, best Belgian cheese. In addition to the national cuisine, the restaurant serves interesting Bhavani Indian delicacies, resisting which is simply impossible despite the fact whether you are a gourmet, or a usual visitor. The restaurant features a separate children's menu, so it is the ideal choice for families.

Besides traditional Belgian beer, waffles, and chocolate, Bruge can offer a range of interesting national delicacies to guests of the city. Tourists on a budget usually like to order French fries that are considered the most popular "street food" in Bruges. Local people started cooking French fries yet in the 16th century. Nowadays, crispy roasted potatoes are available in all local cafes and restaurants specializing in the national cuisine. French fries are served as a garnish to many popular dishes, including mussels that are incredibly popular in Belgium. There are even local cafes that specialize exclusively in cooking French fries.

Beer fans in Bruges will be genuinely delighted with a visit to De Halve Maan. This old brewery has been operating since 1546. It organizes interesting excursions for tourists, during which visitors can find out about secrets of brewing different sorts of beer. Connoisseurs of the foamy drink are recommended to try local Kvak beer during their stay in Bruges. This beer has not only unusual taste but also a very original serving the beer is served in glasses of a particular shape.

National cuisine restaurants in Bruges offer their guests to try a range of traditional dishes with the game. Many of these dishes have been cooked in accordance with unchanged recipes for several centuries. For example, the Huidevettershuis restaurant has several signature dishes, including rabbit roasted in a peculiar way. Local restaurants specializing in the national cuisine also offer delicious, mouthwatering steaks. Menus of the traditional restaurants will pleasantly surprise travelers keen on seafood. They are recommended to try mussels cooked in dozens of ways and the famous fish soup with prawns.

Rabbit stew is a famous gastronomic specialty of Bruges. Locals also like eel stew. Various dishes with chicken meat are also very widespread in the city. It is important to mention that chicken is less popular in other regions of Belgium. Fans of desserts should not forget to visit the Museum of Chocolate in Bruges that is not only one of the biggest venues of its kind in the country but also in the world. The museum's visitors will learn a lot of interesting information about the peculiarities of different kinds of Belgian chocolate and, of course, sample the ever popular dessert. Once the excursion is over, visitors are welcome to purchase fabulous chocolate gifts for their friends and family.

Tradition and Nightlife

Colors of Brugge traditions, festivals, mentality and lifestyle

The residents of the city celebrate their main national holiday on July 21. On this day in 1831 the great King Leopold became the ruler of the kingdom, declaring its independence. Since that time July 21 has become a significant event and the time of conducting various folk festivals, which are traditionally accompanied by lively street performances, festivals and fairs.

Accuracy and diligence have remained one of the main traits of local residents. Starting from ancient times, this place has become widely famous for high quality lace and weapons. It's amazing and surprising that the masters of those time could equally control both thin and fragile materials, and steel. Currently Bruges is a major center for production of electronics, so the local people never cease to amaze visitors with their talents.

Travelers can buy beautiful jewelry as a souvenir in Bruges. It is believed that the local jewelers cut diamonds according to special rules and use the same method of processing gemstones as their ancestors many centuries ago. The local inhabitants are very friendly to tourists who are just captivated by the kindness and hospitality of the city's people.

An important religious holiday called Day of the Holy Blood is celebrated annually in Bruges. The celebration does not have the exact date and depends on what day Easter is celebrated this year. It is believed that local residents started celebrating the Feast of the Holy Blood in 1149 when the Flemish Count brought a valuable relic to the city a vessel with the blood of Jesus Christ. The count won this valuable relic in a crusade. When residents found out about this relic, they turned to the count with a request to bow to the religious shrine. Gradually, the rumors about the precious vessel spread throughout the country and further, attracting pilgrims from different countries to Bruges. Currently over one hundred thousands of pilgrims come to the city on this memorable day. A massive procession is held in the city, the participants of which are dressed in ancient costumes of the clergy and knights.

The city of Bruges is the place where the counterpoint is seen at every step. An amazing combination of the astonishing medieval architecture of Western Europe and modern culture create the unforgettable atmosphere. By the way, did you know that Bruges is also called the "Northern Venice"? The number of channels and waterways flowing into the North Sea can spot Venice itself. Also, people of Bruges enjoy celebrating various holidays and welcome tourists from all over the world. The biggest attention they pay to religious holidays, and one of the most honoured is the Procession of the Holy Blood. It is the considerable religious event making a part of cultural heritage of the country. Annually, tens of thousands of people take part in a solemn procession, putting on suits of ancient knights and monks. This procession represents and reminds about the first crusades when the Flemish count received a sacred the relic of Blood of Christ.

Feest in 't Park, is one of the main events of summer. Every year, at the end of June, in the Bruges central park hundreds of families gather to enjoy time during the event. Tourists are always welcomed to share the joy and fun. During the festival you will be offered to enjoy various entertainments for free, starting from master classes in crafts and finishing with tasting the beer. In the centre of the park you here is a big open-air stage, where musicians from different countries will entertain you. Moreover, you can get a free lesson of folk dances of Belgian, African, Indian and Arab cultures. Within the festival, you have a chance to purchase various crafts and souvenirs on the trade fair. In a gastronomic zone, visitors will be suggested to try national dishes and to buy unusual products.

In the case, you missed Feest in 't Park in June, you will have the chance to have fun during another festival called Moods! It takes place at the end of July and in the first days of August. Within two full weeks, a lot of musical performances and unforgettable fireworks will be established in the most notable places of interest in Bruges like the yard of Beffroi belltower. In a unique environment, you will be able to enjoy the best national and international performances at one of eight evening concerts. Moreover, concerts will take place at Burg Square and the entrance is free.

Accommodations

Extraordinary hotels

Extraordinary hotels best choice for your unusual city break in Brugge

Hotel Fevery

From Brugge center 0.8 km

There are many interesting and peculiar hotels in Bruges. They will be certainly liked by travelers who want to organize a truly unforgettable vacation. Located not far away from the Market Square, Hotel Fevery occupies a beautiful historic building. For many years this hotel has been run by the same family. An important fact Hotel Fevery is an environment conscious hotel. Only natural materials were used during the latest restoration. Guestrooms come with beautiful antique furniture and genuine artworks. The hotel will be liked by travelers who are concerned about their healthy lifestyle every morning they will be treated with fresh fruit and homemade jam.

Hotel Monsieur Ernest

From Brugge center 0.5 km

Guests of the ancient Belgian city have an opportunity to spend several days in a real aristocratic residence. Such an opportunity is offered by Hotel Monsieur Ernest that occupies a unique building of the 14th century. More than 600 years ago the building belonged to one of the richest dukes in the country. Despite such an honorable age, some elements of the original design can be seen even nowadays, including the wooden ladder with forged banisters, arched passages, carved columns and other stone and wood decorations. This magnificent hotel is a great opportunity to see and feel the atmosphere of the historic past of Bruges.

Hotel Maraboe
From Brugge center 0.7 km
Hotel Maraboe is a no less interesting place. The beautiful building of the hotel dates back to the 18th century. Originally, a brewery was located there. Nowadays, the unique hotel offers 14 rooms decorated in modern style. The ground floor of the building was turned into a fantastically looking gym with the arched stone ceiling.

Charlie Rockets Youth Hostel
From Brugge center 0.3 km
The choice of quality hostels and budget hotels is really wide in Bruges. Charlie Rockets Youth Hostel is often called the most unusual and creative hostel in the city. Located just several minutes away from the Market Square, this hostel features truly creative and colorful design. Charlie Rockets Youth Hostel is open in a historic building and

some elements of design, such as fragments of the original wooden carcass, remind visitors that they stay at an antique place. The bar has become a calling card of the hostel. Made in the style of the middle of the 20th century, the bar serves signature cocktails and best sorts of Belgian beer.

B&B Koetshuis
From Brugge center 1 km
B&B Koetshuis remains one of the most secluded and romantic hotels in whole Bruges. It has only two charming guestrooms open in a wing of an old mansion, which is hidden by a lush garden from prying eyes. The hotel is designed in accordance with traditions of the past, and so it will be a wonderful destination for a romantic vacation. Every day, guests of the hotel will be able to relax in the picturesque garden in the daytime, and in the evening they are welcome at the lounge bar that serves best Belgian beer. There are many interesting sights near the hotel, including the Church of Our Lady, Minnewater Park and an ancient castle.

B&B Contrast
From Brugge center 0.6 km
you will find B&B Contrast hotel not far from Grand Place Square, surrounded by a beautiful garden. The hotel is open in a restored single-storey building and offers only 5 comfortable guestrooms. The hotel looks very catchy because of its architectural style it feels like the hotel makes a unified whole with the nature surrounding it. Many

guestrooms come with a private wooden terrace; there is also an originally looking glass covered gallery at the hotel. The garden surrounding the hotel deserves the closest attention besides interesting landscape decorations, there is a rich collection of sculptures. Some guestrooms of this unusual hotel offer charming views of the canal.

Stylish design-hotels

Stylish weekend in Brugge collection of top unique boutique hotels

B&B Lady Jane
From Brugge center 0.7 km
Quite a small, but absolutely charming B&B Lady Jane show on the map is located in a historic building. However, its design is very stylish and far from a classic. Each guestroom comes with original individual design, but all of them are equally comfortable and will be a great choice for travelers seeking a pleasant stay in Bruges. Guests of the hotel are welcome to attend special wine and beer sampling sessions, during which they will be offered to try more than 30 sorts of finest Belgian beer, including famous Duvel, Westmalle, Karmeliet, Leffe and Hoegaarden. The sessions take place at the private wine cellar of the hotel.

Exclusive Guesthouse Bonifacius
From Brugge center 0.4 km

Boutique hotel Exclusive Guesthouse Bonifacius show on the map is the place that fully reflects the wish of the owners to create a charming and beautiful place. Guestrooms come with antique furniture and luxurious textiles, posh decorations and genuine artworks. The roof of the building was transformed into a sunny terrace, where guests of the hotel are welcome to enjoy magnificent views of the city canals. When it's too cold to stay on the terrace, move to the warm hall with fireplace. Hospitable owner and staff of the hotel do everything to please guests and make them feel comfortable.

Montanus Hotel

Stylish Montanus Hotel show on the map is located right in the middle of a city park. The hotel is located in the main mansion and a smaller cottage. Travelers will be delighted with luxurious and stylish interiors that were skillfully decorated by a designer team. The 17th-century style of the white living room is worth a separate mention. Nowadays, the room was transformed into a charming bar. The peaceful atmosphere of a city park and relaxation with a cup of tea on a beautiful terrace promise travelers to be nothing but mesmerizing.

Floris Karos

Floris Karos show on the map is one of the newest hotels in Bruges. The charming and unforgettable architecture of the building adds to the comfort and peaceful atmosphere. Fully refurbished guestrooms of the hotel feature sophisticated and exclusive style. There is a private garden in the territory of the hotel, which is a great destination after a busy day full of sightseeing and exploration of the city. When it's cold outside, there is nothing better than to sit near the fireplace in the cozy lounge bar of the hotel.

Maison Bousson
From Brugge center 1.2 km
Fans of modern style may be fond of Maison Bousson show on the map mini hotel. It is located not far from the centre of Bruges and is open on the site of a former quarry. The hotel has only three guest rooms made in light shades and decorated with designer furniture and interesting artworks. Besides standard paintings, one can see various colorful textiles, interesting collages, handmade items and elegant vases with flowers. The design hotel also has a wellness centre with a swimming pool.

Den Witten Leeuw
From Brugge center 0.7 km
Many popular hotels in Bruges are located in historic buildings. Den Witten Leeuw show on the map is no exception. It is also open in an eye-catching building with centuries-old history. This hotel is very popular with couples, who enjoy staying in one of the three beautiful twin rooms with romantic design. Large white beds with canopies, posh textiles, genuine antiquities and artworks are the main design elements of this magnificent hotel. Many original decorations have

been preserved in the hotel, such as historic beam joints and mansard ceilings.

Hotels with history

Preserved history of Brugge: long-standing and historical hotels

De Orangerie

From Brugge center 0.2 km

Spectacular De Orangerie show on the map Hotel is located in a unique historic mansion, the history of which starts yet in the 15th century. Initially, a monastery stood on the site of the mansion, in 1873 it was rebuilt into a palace. After a thorough restoration it was decided to keep the style of the 19th century, so at this hotel guests will see original marble floors, oak tree doors, skillful fretwork, genuine artworks, fine china and silver tableware of the 18th 19th centuries. The refined elegance of past centuries remains the calling card of De Orangerie.

NH Brugge

From Brugge center 0.8 km

With its original stained-glass windows, brick fireplaces and old beam ceilings, historic NH Brugge show on the map resembles a 17th-century monastery. Guestrooms are mostly made in French countryside style. The stone terrace of the hotel is an ideal place to have a cup of coffee in the morning or relax and enjoy a delicious cocktail in the evening. The hotel's staff is very friendly, hospitable and tries to do their best to make sure guests feel comfortable and are pleased with their stay at NH Brugge.

The Pand
From Brugge center 0.3 km
The Pand show on the map is another wonderful historic hotel, which is located in an 18th-century mansion. The family, which owns the hotel, is keen on art, so the refined taste of the owners has reflected in design and atmosphere of the hotel. Romantic guestrooms come with large beds with canopies, premium textiles, antique furniture, and are decorated with valuable artworks. A peaceful inner yard with a charming fountain, a library with a great collection of old books, a wonderful bar the atmosphere of elegance and comfort reigns throughout the hotel. On demand of travelers, fine breakfasts on silver tableware and premium champagne can be served directly in guestrooms.

Huis T Schaep
From Brugge center 0.6 km
Huis T Schaep show on the map is located on one of the central streets in Bruges. The hotel occupies an eye-catching 17th-century building. Upon entering the hotel, you will be amazed at its unforgettable charm of the past. Guestrooms at Huis T Schaep come with posh wooden beds with high bed rests and canopies, genuine antique furniture, magnificent paintings by famous Belgian artists and other valuable and beautiful items. There is a breakfast hall on the ground

floor of the building, where it's hard not to notice a marvelous buffet with antique fine china.

Vakantie Logies Hollywood
From Brugge center 0.7 km
Vakantie Logies Hollywood show on the map is one of the most interesting historic hotels in Bruges. As it is not hard to guess from its name, the hotel's design is dedicated to Hollywood. It is located in a typical historic building with the preserved original wooden carcass. Besides antique furniture, the hotel exhibits an interesting collection of vintage photographs. In the photos, you will see Hollywood stars of the middle of the 20th century, retro filmmaking equipment and interesting on set moments. When it's warm outside, guests of this wonderful hotel are welcome to relax on an open terrace, where they will be treated with best sorts of Belgian beer.

Luxury accommodation

Top places to stay in Brugge most luxury and fashionable hotels

Die Swaene
From Brugge center 0.2 km
Die Swaene show on the map is located on a pebble pavement near a picturesque canal. The hotel is surrounded by historic buildings that only add to the heritage of the area. The main hall of Die Swaene has retained the atmosphere of the past and contains some true gems, like the elegantly painted ceiling created in 1779. Refined and

luxurious guestrooms feature classic design with romantic elements and offer wonderful views of the canal. The new building of the hotel, Canal House, has some absolutely stunning guestrooms built on the sea level. Traditions and comfort of guests are highly valued at Die Swaene, so the hotel proves its respectable title of one of the most luxurious and romantic places in the city.

De Tuilerieen
From Brugge center 0.3 km
The next hotel in our list, De Tuilerieen show on the map, enjoys an amazing location in a 15th-century mansion with an eye-catching traditional façade. Small and charming hall of the hotel is decorated with comfortable leather sofas and antiquities. It's a miracle that during its long history the hotel has retained its original atmosphere of romance and heritage. All guestrooms, big and small ones, are made in a similar style and feature mansard ceilings, arched ceiling beams and wooden floors. The hotel's bar is a no less charming place with a cozy fireplace. Owners of the hotel wanted to create historic accommodation with excellent service and its own peculiar style, and they succeeded in that.

Grand Hotel Casselbergh
From Brugge center 0.2 km
Elegant Grand Hotel Casselbergh show on the map is located in three medieval buildings. The face of the hotel features original decorations that date back to the 13th and 16th centuries. The hotel's design is

mostly classical, very elegant and contains many antique details. Luxurious rooms feature beautiful views of the canal. The hotel's lounge zone is not only a good place to pamper yourself with delicious light snacks and drinks; it's a magnificent historic place with a fireplace and a library. Fans of ultimate comfort and prestigious places will like Grand Hotel Casselbergh as it is often called the most prestigious hotel in whole Bruges.

Hotel Relais Bourgondisch Cruyce A Luxe Worldwide Hotel
From Brugge center 0.2 km
Absolutely marvelous Hotel Relais Bourgondisch Cruyce A Luxe Worldwide Hotel show on the map amazes travelers right from the start the magnificent façade of this boutique hotel is made of bricks and wood and is decorated with stained-glass windows. The location of the hotel between two canals is no less amazing. Inside travelers will find luxurious textiles, elegant antiquities, and precious artworks. By the way, this hotel can be seen in the famous movie "In Bruges". Those, who have seen the movie, will surely want to visit this miraculous city and book a room at Hotel Relais Bourgondisch Cruyce.

Heritage Hotel
From Brugge center 0.2 km
Heritage Hotel show on the map is an ultra-luxury hotel in Bruges. After a thorough restoration, an ancient mansion was turned into a hotel that deserves the highest praise. Twenty elegantly decorated rooms in mostly classic style will fit any taste and demands. Having

stayed at Heritage Hotel, you will want to return there again and again!

Charming Brugge
From Brugge center 1.2 km
Travellers, who wish to stay at an elite hotel, will like Charming Brugge show on the map mini-hotel that is located in a beautiful building constructed in 1926. This hotel has only 4 posh guestrooms with luxurious wooden décor, branded furniture and a state-of-art lighting system. Only best antique items were used in décor of public spaces. The hotel has a spa centre with sauna, massage rooms and an outdoor pool in the inner yard.

Romantic hotels
Brugge for couples in love best hotels for intimate escape, wedding or honeymoon
Relais Bourgondisch Cruyce
From Brugge center 0.2 km
Let yourself be charmed by the most romantic hotel in Europe. Relais Bourgondisch Cruyce show on the map is elegantly decorated with valuable antiquities, exclusive artworks, premium furniture and magnificent flower bouquets. The hotel offers simply mesmerizing views of the historic city centre and will help you enjoy an absolutely unforgettable vacation in the magic city of Bruges.

Jacquemine Luxury Guesthouse and Art Gallery
From Brugge center 0.4 km

Jacquemine Luxury Guesthouse and Art Gallery show on the map offers travellers to stay in romantic and elegant guestrooms with beautiful design, in which guests will find a comfortable leather sofa, flat TV, teapots and a coffee machine. The hotel is surrounded by a charming Japanese garden that borders with a canal. This is a fantastic choice for a great family weekend!

Maison Bousson
From Brugge center 1.2 km
Located in a peaceful area, Maison Bousson show on the map is a small boutique hotel with beautifully decorated elegant rooms, which are nothing but perfect for a romantic vacation. Various facilities, such as an outdoor swimming pool, will make your stay at Maison Bousson very comfortable. Active travellers are offered to make a bicycle ride in the hotel's garden. When it's cold outside, there's nothing better than to relax in a cozy hall near the fireplace. The atmosphere of calmness, peace and comfort will surround you during your stay at romantic Bruges.

Brugsche Suites Luxury Guesthouse
From Brugge center 1 km
Brugsche Suites Luxury Guesthouse show on the map is a charming mansion that has only three stylish suites. The rooms feature all modern amenities including a spacious bathroom and a living room with a fireplace. Decorated with antique furniture, the suites have the charm and appeal of a rich house. The hospitable atmosphere and

luxurious furnishing of this high-class guesthouse will please even most discerning travellers. Brugsche Suites Luxury Guesthouse will be a perfect choice for travellers who seek serene and calm pastime.

Martins Relais
From Brugge center 0.4 km
Couples, who are used to staying in high-class hotels, may like Martins Relais show on the map. This luxurious hotel is located near a canal and occupies a complex of five fully restored historic buildings that were constructed more than 300 years ago. At the hotel, travellers will find amazing posh guestrooms decorated with antique furniture and retro textiles. Without a doubt, suites are the most romantic place at Martins Relais as they feature charming views of the canal. There is a cozy bar with an amazing choice of cocktails and signature drinks at the hotel. However, travellers are not limited to facilities present at the hotel as only a short walk separates them from the Market Square and central streets.

Casa Romantico
From Brugge center 0.4 km
Villa-hotel Casa Romantico show on the map is an ideal place for couples who seek privacy and serenity. This hotel is also open in a beautiful historic building and is surrounded by a lush garden. Besides charming guestrooms, guests of the hotel are welcome to rest in a cozy inner yard with wooden terraces and an outdoor swimming pool. The guestrooms look slightly different, but all of them feature

beautiful handmade wooden furniture and premium textiles. The most unusual room is located on the mansard and has beautiful beam ceiling. Finally, there is a nice bar at the hotel, which is a great place in the evening.

Legendary hotels

Brugge legends. Famous hotels glorified by history or celebrities

good morning bruges Relais Bourgondisch Cruyce Hotel had been a popular hotel before the famous movie "In Bruges" came out. Nowadays, one needs to book rooms in advance to be able to stay there. The wood and stone façade and large stained-glass windows of the building beautifully reflect in water of the nearby canal. All 16 guestrooms of the hotel are furnished with vintage antique items. Main characters of the movie, Ken and Ray, stayed at room 10. They considered this city a real fairy-tale, and it's hard to disagree with them. In order to reach this exceptional hotel, one needs to cross the charming Bonifacius Bridge. Upon entering the hotel, guests are greeted by the family of artist David De Graef. Travelers are offered to stay at magnificent rooms that are still reminiscent of the medieval period in the history of Bruges. The hotel is so exceptional and unique that it was selected by the family of King of Belgium, who stayed there during the honeymoon.

Kempinski Hotel Dukes Palace

From Brugge center 0.4 km
Kempinski Hotel Dukes Palace show on the map is located in a fully restored palace of the 15th century. The palace was built by Philip the Good, the Duke of Burgundy specifically for his marriage ceremony with Isabel de Aragon. Magnificent interior of the palace is made mostly in bold violet, bronze and green shades that can be found on ancient tapestries and only underline the glorious past of the building. Gardens of the palace are no less breath-taking with their ancient sculptures by famous masters. Elegance in every detail only proves that this historic place is worth the highest praise.

Hotel Jan Brito
From Brugge center 0.3 km
The former residence of baroness de Geiy is now known as Hotel Jan Brito show on the map. The building of the hotel is protected by UNESCO, so all restorations were very thoughtful and their main aim was to keep the original design and look of the building. Travelers are welcome to admire the beauty of antique marble fireplaces, paintings and the oak ladder. Guestrooms feature the style of different epochs, but all of them reflect the atmosphere of the past. While at the hotel, don't forget to visit a romantic inner yard of Renaissance period and a hundred-year-old beech that grows there. Despite its historic look, Hotel Jan Brito is a luxurious hotel with modern services.

Relais & Châteaux Hotel Heritage

Photo of Relais & Château Hotel Heritage, Bruges Travellers, who find the idea of living in a hotel with rich history appealing, are recommended to pay attention to Relais & Château Hotel Heritage. This hotel is located in a magnificent building constructed in 1869. Initially, the building belonged to one of rich inhabitants of Bruges. Later, the building was transformed into a bank and nowadays it's a hotel with 22 unique guestrooms that would suite even a king. Giant beds with crispy white blankets, carpets with interesting patterns, old paintings in heavy frames, crystal chandeliers you will see valuable antiques simply everywhere in this amazing hotel. By the way, there is a 14th-century wine cellar at the hotel, which has survived from the original building.

Shopping in Brugge

Shopping in Brugge authentic goods, best outlets, malls and boutiques

A leisurely stroll along Walplein street is the best way to start shopping spree in Bruges. It is a very beautiful historic street, which has preserved many spectacular buildings in national style. Nowadays, interesting shops are located in these picturesque houses. You can buy handmade crafts, fresh local food, and wonderful beer from local breweries. On this street there are several colourful national restaurants. In summer they equip spacious lovely terraces at the door.

Flea Market located by the canal is a real city's sight. Many tourists come here in search of original vintage souvenirs. It is here, that you can buy a lot of unique objects of the past. Here they sell beautiful old furniture, paintings and books, old porcelain crafts. You can bind walking around the market with a rest in local restaurants, where visitors are offered traditional fried sausages and delicious beer.

For many, shopping in Bruges is associated with a local chocolate tasting at all times. Those who have a sweet tooth should include a visit to the Chocolate Line confectionery in their program, where they can taste the most popular and original sorts of Belgian chocolate. It sells beautiful figured chocolate. You can taste exotic sorts of chocolate with pepper and spices, as well as classic sorts with nuts and fruit additions. This is a candy store with an open-plan kitchen, so all customers can follow the work of confectioners. Luxurious chocolate is sold by weight. Customers will always have an opportunity to purchase a jar of exclusive chocolate massage cream.

In Bruges, you will find a lot of original souvenir shops selling thematic articles for lovers of beer. De Bier Tempel store remains the best one in this category for many years. It is located next to the Market Square. In this store a huge choice of popular sorts of beer is presented, yet, they sell beer steins, lighters, magnets and other souvenirs with beer symbols. Here, you can find excellent gift bags, and taste the most popular varieties of foam drink.

In the city there is also a specialty store for cheese enthusiasts. It is Diksmuids Boterhuis. In this trading pavilion over a hundred kinds of cheeses are presented, among which you will find unique domestic varieties, and very rare ones, which are more costly. Gourmets will definitely find some good old pampering for themselves. You can taste cheses before purchasing. This store is also mainly focused on tourists, that's why some sorts of cheese are traditionally sold in beautiful gift boxes.

Another interesting symbol of Bruges is lace. Numerous historical lace workshops are located all over the city. Bruges Kantcentrum (the Lace Centre) is a famous city's attraction. It is located in an old 15th-century building. Here, well-known local lacemakers present their works. You can buy incredibly beautiful memorable gifts for yourself and your loved ones. Thematic exhibitions and master classes are often held in this trade pavillion. In Bruges, as in any major tourist city, there is a huge choice of classic clothing stores and shopping centers. But it's not necessary to limit a touristic program by shopping expeditions only for such stores.

Tourist Tips

Preparing your trip to Brugge: advices & hints things to do and to obey
1. Weather in Bruges is quite changeable and cold. Even in summer the temperature rarely rises above +21°C. Tourists are recommended

to take some warm clothes with them and make long walks only with an umbrella, because rain can start here really suddenly.

2. Those, who plan to travel around the city, can buy a special ticket. It can be valid for one day only or a certain number of trips.

3. Guests are not recommended to rent a car to travel using it on narrow streets of the city as it will be very problematic. The city has only several major car parks which are located in the central area. Bicycle will become the best alternative to a car here.

4. Travelers, who plan to attend various tours and museums, should consider purchasing Brugge City Card. It provides discounts on visiting main museums the city, its public transportation, and bicycle rental. It will help you to save up to 200 euros. The card can be purchased for 48 or 72 hours. Moreover, travelers under 26 years will get a discount for this purchase.

5. Tips are included in the bills of almost all restaurants and cafes, so leaving additional money for waiter is not necessary.

6. It is not recommended to discuss such themes vibrant historical events, local culture and history with the locals. Many of them are very sensitive and may be offended because of a careless phrase. The royal family is another taboo subject for conversation.

7. Despite the fact that many customs and traditions of the local people may recall you the traditions of the French, you should never compare their culture with other countries.

8. The locals are very friendly to tourists who try to speak their native language, but are very offended when visitors try to copy their accent.

Brussels

Sightseeing

Sightseeing in Brussels what to see. Complete travel guide
If you come to Brussels, it may simply turn out that you will physically have not enough time for visiting all the sights, monuments and historical buildings of this city. Atomium is known as the symbol of modern Brussels. The sight was projected by A. Waterkeyn for the 1958World's Fair in Brussels. The spheres of Atomium symbolize atoms in a model of an iron crystal, which is enlarged in 165 billion times. The tubes that connect the molecules of iron symbolize the connecting strength. Recently, Atomium has undergone a large restoration. For example, the aluminium facing was changed for a non-rusting one.

> The Grand Place:. The Grand Place, or Grotte Markt in Dutch, was almost totally ruined by the French artillery in 1695, only the City Hall remained untouched. The reconstruction of the square started without any delay and after this the Grand Place turned into one of

the most beautiful squares in the world. The front of every building is unique, but it doesn't prevent the square from looking harmoniously and laconically. The Grand Place is surrounded by the City Hall, The Royal House and The Guild Houses with their fabulous golden fronts in the Flemish style. The Brewers' Guild House is the location of the Museum of Beer and The Royal Palace hosts the exhibition of the National Museum.

> Cinquantenaire Park:. Cinquantenaire Park is an ideal place for travellers, who would like to spend their free time far from stress and noise of big city, and who would like to learn something new. This park was created for the anniversary of the independence of Brussels in accordance with the project of Leopold II. The marvellous triumphal arch is the main distinguishing feature of the park. Famous French Arc de Triomphe was the prototype of this arc. In Cinquantenaire Park you will find many interesting museums, such as the Autoworld Museum, the Royal Museum of Fine Art and the Museum of the Army. This beautiful park is simply the best place for making an unhurried walk and enjoying the beauty of nature.

> St. Michael and Gudula Cathedral:. St. Michael and Gudula Cathedral connects the uptown and the downtown. Its two obtuse towers remind of the Cathedral of Notre-Dame. Even Victor Hugo called it a true gothic cathedral. The process of building of the church started in the beginning of the 13th century, and it was finished only in the end

of the 15th century. Because of this St. Michael and Gudula Cathedral has the elements of both early and late gothic styles. The building is 108 meters tall, 50 meters wide and the distance between the highest towers and the ground is about 69 meters. The cathedral has become home to approximately 1200 precious paintings. St. Michael and Gudula Cathedral wasn't restored for a long time, and after many centuries its stone-work became very dark. However, the cathedral underwent a painstaking restoration, and now everyone can enjoy its beauty in original white color.

> The Royal Castle of Laken:. Thanks to Leopold II the Royal Castle of Laken strikes visitors with its richness and gorgeousness. Leopold II was constantly widening the territory of the castle by buying housing estates from his peasants. The castle has become the residence of the Royal Family of Belgium since the 19th century. While walking in the park you'll surely see various places of interest, such as the Royal Palace, the China Tower, the central dome of the royal greenhouses or the China Hall.

> The Royal Palace:. The Royal Palace is one of the most fabulous official buildings in Brussels. It symbolizes Belgium monarchy. This is the place where the king fulfils his duty as the head of the country, solves governmental questions and holds audiences. Everyone can visit the Royal Palace and its terraces from the 21st of July till the beginning of September.

Top Sightseeing

Top architectural sightseeing and landmarks of Brussels ideas on city exploration routes

This review is a great opportunity to look at architectural landmarks of Brussels from a new perspective namely, from the sky. Click the video to enjoy a 3D flight over the architectural ensemble of Brussels and to look at the most interesting landmarks in detail at Brussels Town Hall, Atomium, Law Courts, La Monnaie, Royal Museum of Armed Forces and many others. Below you will find the most amusing historic facts and professional photographs of every famous sightseeing in Brussels.

Brussels Town Hall, Brussels

Facts: » The Brussels Town Hall is one of the most beautiful buildings in the city, which is the symbol of Brussels.

» The 5-meter statue of the Archangel Michael, the patron saint of Brussels, throwing devil is installed at the 96-meter Gothic Tower.

» The oldest part of the town hall was built in 1420, and the other part of the building was completed a little later (in 1450).

» Facade of the Hall is decorated with numerous statues of nobles, saints, and allegorical figures. In fact, existing sculpture are only reproductions, and originals are kept in the House of the King.

» The Town Hall is still used as the residence of the mayor and is available for tours.

Atomium, Brussels

Facts: » Atomium is another great attraction of Brussels. This building was constructed for the opening of the World Expo 1958; that's the symbol of the atomic age and the peaceful use of nuclear energy.

» Construction of the Atomium is decorated with nine atoms united in a root fragment of the crystal lattice of iron magnified 165 billion times.

» CNN called this building the most bizarre one in Europe.

» The height of the entire structure is 102 meters, and the weight of the structure is about 2,400 tons. The diameter of each of the nine areas of construction is 18 meters.

» Six areas are available for visit. In the mid-pipe of the building, connecting the central sphere there is an elevator. It's capable to lift the visitors to the restaurant and the viewing platform located in the highest ball of Atomium in 25 seconds.

Law Courts, Brussels

Facts: » The Law Courts is the building of the state court in Brussels constructed between 1866 and 1883.

» Dimensions of the building are impressive: 160 meters long and 150 meters wide. The height of Law Courts reaches 142 meters.

» The Law Courts is the largest building constructed in the 19th century.

» Eight courtyards with a total area of 6,000 square meters, 27 large court rooms and 245 smaller courtrooms, and many other rooms are situated in the complex.

» The Law Courts is decorated with numerous sculptures of famous ancient lawyers, philosophers and orators such as Demosthenes, Lycurgus of Sparta, Cicero, Ulpian and others.

La Monnaie, Brussels

Facts: » La Monnaie has being among the leading European opera venues in recent decades.

» In 2011, La Monnaie was considered the best of the major opera houses.

» Festivals of theatrical performances and various creative competitions are often held there.

» Tours around the premises and theater workshops are held on Saturdays.

» The building of la Monnaie was built in 1855; that was the third construction for the theater. Auditorium houses 1,150 people, and the foyer is designed for 250 seats.

Royal Museum of Armed Forces, Brussels

Facts: » The Royal Museum of Armed Forces is the military history museum opened in 1923.

» The museum's collection is one of the largest military collections in the world.

» The museum has the separate pavilion of 100 meters long, which displays military aircrafts from the very first models of airplanes to modern jets. In addition, the museum even has a special tank yard.

» A lot of the exhibits are devoted to the first and second world wars.

» The museum has a huge collection of weapons, including cold and small arms, artillery, tanks, cars, planes, uniforms and equipment of the soldiers, and objects of military life. The museum also represents a variety of weapons dating back to the Middle Ages.

Chapel Church, Brussels

Facts: » The Chapel Church is one of the oldest churches in Brussels, the first mention of which dates back to 1134 year. During its long history the church has undergone many changes; it has repeatedly been destroyed and rebuilt.

» There are graves of local nobility and famous people inside the church.

» Nowadays, the Chapel Church is the parish church of the Polish Catholic community in Brussels.

» You can see the entire collection of paintings, sculptures and stained glass inside the temple.

» The church regularly hosts a variety of concerts. It's open to visitors all year round.

Halle Gate, Brussels

Facts: » Halle Gate is the medieval gate and the only surviving fragment of the city wall of Brussels.

» Currently the building is used as a museum.

» The exact date of construction is unknown, but according to archival documents construction refers to the period between 1357 and 1373.

» In addition to defense and customs, in the 17th century the gate began to carry out the function of the prison.

» Currently gate is used as a branch of the Royal museums of Art and History. Exposition of the museum is devoted to the history of the gate itself, ancient weapons and Medieval history of Brussels.

Church of Our Blessed Lady, Brussels

Facts: » The Church of Our Blessed Lady is one of the clearest examples of temples built in the late Gothic style.

» The Church was built in the period from 1400 to 1594. It's located near Small Sablon Park that was laid in honor of the great men of the sixteenth century.

» The church building is decorated with beautiful stained glass windows; bright interior lighting is turned on in the night.

» Since its construction in 1784, the church has being serving as the burial place for noble aristocratic families.

» The church is famous for its numerous sculptures adorning the facade of the building, its grounds and interior.

Architecture and Monuments

Excursion tour in Brussels. Top architecture monuments, castles, temples and palaces

Let's continue our virtual walk in Brussels and its most prominent architecture monuments. This time, we will focus on such breathtaking sights as Cathedral of St. Michael and St. Gudula, Basilica of the Sacred Heart, Royal Palace, Royal Palace of Laeken, Saint Jacques sur Coudenberg and many others. For many people, the cultural and historical vibe of these monuments defines the atmosphere of not only Brussels, but also Belgium in general. We will make a virtual 3D tour to every monument, look at it from a bird's eye view, and browse the most interesting facts that have defined the history of Brussels. The photo gallery and maps are the cherry on the cake!

Cathedral of St. Michael and St. Gudula, Brussels

Facts:

» The Cathedral of St. Michael and St. Gudula is one of the main attractions of Brussels, and the clearest example of Gothic architecture.

» The building of the cathedral is a symmetrical composition with two towers, within which there is a long staircase opening onto the terrace that is 64 meters high. The terrace offers a magnificent view of the city.

» The Cathedral has four doors decorated with wrought-reliefs and statues of saints. There is a huge stained glass above the main entrance.

» Stained glasses decorating the cathedral were created in the 16th century by Jan Haq and in 18-19th century by Jean-Baptiste Kaproner.

» The cathedral houses the mausoleum of the Belgian national hero Frederic de Merode.

Basilica of the Sacred Heart, Brussels

Facts: » The Catholic Basilica of the Sacred Heart is dedicated to the Sacred Heart of Jesus. It was inspired by the eponymous basilica in Paris.

» This shrine is the sixth area of the Roman Catholic Church in the world.

» The church is the large structure with two towers and a green copper dome towering 89 meters above the ground. The length of the building is almost 165 meters.

» In total the church can accommodate up to 2,000 people.

» The basilica houses a restaurant, a Catholic radio station, theater, two museums, and a place of training cavers and climbers.

Royal Palace, Brussels

Facts: » The Royal Palace is the official residence of the Belgian monarch situated in the heart of the capital.

» At present the royal family palace is used mainly as a venue for formal events.

» Every summer, the Royal Palace is traditionally open to the public. You can get inside the palace and see its galleries and chambers for free.

» Throne Hall with its grand decor, a wonderful mirror room, the ceiling of which is decorated with winged scarab beetles, and the Imperial Room with gorgeous golden flower pots, where plants of eleven colors, one for each province of Belgium, are the most notable places.

» The palace also houses the museum of Bellevue, which was once a hotel accommodating many famous people. Now that's the museum of history of Belgium.

Royal Palace of Laeken, Brussels

Facts: » The Royal Palace of Laeken is the residence of the Belgian royal family, where it currently resides.

» The building of the palace was built in 1781-1785 in the style of Classicism.

» The Royal Palace of Laeken is also famous for its territory boasting a magnificent park, a lake, the Royal Conservatory, a golf course and various pavilions.

» The park has two buildings unusual for Belgium style. Those are the Chinese pavilion and the Japanese tower that appeared here after Leopold II visited the World's Fair in Paris in 1900; there he saw pavilions of different countries, so he wanted to decorate his park.

» Opposite the park there is the neo-Gothic Church of Our Lady in Laeken with the crypt serving as the burial place of the royal family.

» Unfortunately, the palace itself is closed to the public, but the park, pavilions and conservatory are open for everyone.

Saint Jacques sur Coudenberg, Brussels

Facts: » Saint Jacques sur Coudenberg was built in the second half of the 18th century in neoclassical style. It looks a lot like a palace or ancient Greek temple.

» The building is decorated with a wooden tower that serves as a belfry. It has four bells.

» Balustrades of the cathedral are decorated with three large statues; the statue of St. James can be seen in the center.

» Between French conquests the church was converted into a Temple of Reason, and later in the Temple of the Law. However, in 1802 it was re-consecrated as a Catholic.

» Today, Saint Jacques sur Coudenberg is the part of an ensemble of nine neoclassical buildings surrounding the perimeter of the Royal Square. The equestrian statue of Godefroid de Bouillon, who led the first Crusade, is in the center of the square.

Church of St. Catherine, Brussels

Facts: » The building of the Church of St. Catherine was constructed in 1854-1874 years. Its facade combines Gothics with Romanesque features.

» The interior is very bright due to the white plaster on the walls; it's designed in neo-Renaissance style.

» The belfry standing apart from the temple is actually much older than the Church of St. Catherine. It has been preserved from the old church, which stood on that site previously.

» The main altar of the church is decorated with painting The Assumption of St. Catherine.

Family and Kids

Family trip to Brussels with children. Ideas on where to go with your child

In Brussels, there are many prospects for an unforgettable holiday with children. Upon arrival, many travellers prefer to visit Brussels Aquarium. This is a place, where they will be able to see an amazing collection of marine creatures, many of which are quite rare. One can spend hours watching them, and in the largest aquarium, there are the most dangerous animals of the deep sea sharks. The aquarium is open every day, and guests can either pick a guided tour or choose to walk independently among the huge aquariums and admire their inhabitants.

To visit Brussels and fail to attend the local Museum of Cocoa and Chocolate is an unforgivable mistake for tourists with children and all sweet tooths. This thematic museum features a very interesting and informative exhibition that is dedicated to the process of making chocolate back in the time of Maya. In addition to an educating excursion, guests of the museum are welcome to attend fascinating master classes, during which they will be able to see how masters work and even learn how to make their favorite chocolate sweets.

While in the city, don't forget to visit the Museum of Natural Sciences, which also enjoys well-deserved popularity among travelers with children. An exhibition devoted to dinosaurs and other prehistoric inhabitants of the planet will be particularly interesting for kids. It is important to note that the museum often hosts special excursions for groups of children of various ages. During such excursions, kids will learn how civilizations were developing on our planet, and will also see unique artifacts discovered by researchers.

Bruparck is the most famous and popular amusement park in Brussels. It can be interesting to spend days on end there. It will really take more than one day to try all attractions of this amusement park in action. There are special playgrounds for kids, and older children and adults will enjoy extreme attractions. Another attractive feature of the amusement park is a roofed water park located on its territory. This is a real tropical paradise with beautiful pools and colorful slides. The water park works all year round.

Toy Museum can be called the most "childish" landmark of Brussels. The museum exhibits a unique collection of old toys, and the age of some items is more than a hundred years. Such a number of dolls and teddy bears can hardly be seen in any other museum in the world. Children will certainly be pleased with the fact that literally all the exhibits of the museum can be touched, and some can even be bought.

The Mini Europe Park is another attractive place for family rest. This is an interesting miniature park, which in fact is a real open-air museum. In this park, there are copies of world famous attractions, including Venice in miniature with its charming canals, the Eiffel Tower, the main symbol of London Big Ben, as well as many other world famous attractions and architectural landmarks.

In the immediate vicinity of Brussels, travellers will find Walibi Amusement Park a real fairy-tale country, in which everyone will find a suitable place to relax. In this complex there are an amusement park, playrooms and playgrounds for small children, as well as a wonderful water park and even a small farm. Every day interesting shows are organized for visitors, in which they will see marine animals, and performances with exotic birds have become the calling card of the park.

Unusual Weekend

How to spend top weekend in Brussels ideas on extraordinary attractions and sites

If it feels like you've already seen all notable landmarks and places of interest in Brussels and now want to see something new, it's high time to explore wondrous hidden sights of the city that only some tourists manage to find. Maison la Bellone is one of these places. This is an amazingly beautiful building in Baroque style, the construction of which was finished in 1967. The full address of this building is Rue de Flandre 46; because of newer buildings, this masterpiece is not well seen during an ordinary walk. Nowadays, the building belongs to a local culture centre and is often used to host various concerts and other important events. However, travellers can admire the beauty of the well-preserved façade and the inner yard free of charge. To do that, simply knock on the door and explain your purpose to a watchman.

There are many amazing cafes and restaurants in the city. Without a doubt, they are a great place to spend a couple of hours and rest, but how about making an after lunch rest in a car salon? Not far away from the city, on Grand Sablon Island, you will find Mercedes House that sells newest car models of the famous brand. That is not the only advantage of that place as there is a wonderful bar in the salon, where visitors are welcome to relax in a calm setting and at the same time enjoy the look of posh cars.

Do you like walking and wish to admire the unforgettable panoramic views of Brussels? If so, then early in the morning you are recommended to head to Place Poelaert. Not everyone knows that the square offers magnificent views of the city. There is a high hill on the square, and if you reach its top, the view will be even more breath-taking. If you are not in the mood of climbing yourself, use the glass elevator that is located not far from the Palace of Justice.

Do you think you've been at all most interesting museums in Brussels? That might be a mistake because most probably you haven't visited Musee des Egouts or the Museum of Sewers. Travellers are allowed to visit this underground museum only once a week, so it's better to find out its work schedule in advance. Moreover, travellers must be accompanied by a guide in order to enter. The museum is located on Porte d Anderlecht, namely, below this street, and its exhibition is dedicated to the history of Brussels sewers, one of the oldest sewers in the world.

One more popular "open air museum" can be found on Place Grand Sablon. This is the antiquity market that works on that square. It is considered the best antiquity market in the country. Here visitors can find really unique items and, what's more important, to buy them at reasonable prices. Besides antiquity shops, there are shops of famous chocolate masters, charming bars and restaurants at the square, and even a beautiful park for travellers who want to relax in a peaceful place among old trees.

Fans of shopping are recommended to visit one of the most unusual shops in whole Brussels Western Shop. This is a charming shop located on Bd.Adolphe Street. The shop is made in cowboy style and is decorated with unusual mannequins of Native Americans. The owner usually greets visitors himself, also dressed as a cowboy. The shop sells interesting souvenirs dedicated to Wild West and exhibits some very interesting items like old black and white photos and other antiques. By the way, the owner allows customers making photos with the mannequins and sculptures installed in the trading pavilion.

Cultural Sights

Culture of Brussels. Places to visit old town, temples, theaters, museums and palaces

Brussels offers to its guests visits to most unusual memorials, interesting museums and theaters. Among the unique monuments of our time we simply can't fail to mention Atomium. This monument is a huge model of iron molecule. The monument was built in 1958 in honor of the World's Fair. The height of the model is 122 meters. Visitors are allowed to use elevator that will bring you to a specially equipped area, where you can enjoy panoramic views of the city.

Travellers will get introduced with the history of the city in Civic Museum, the collections of which include numerous historical artifacts and art objects. The museum is located in a beautiful historical building that features Gothic Revival style. Young visitors will also find much interesting in visiting another cultural institution Museum of Natural Science. Among the exhibits of this place you will find rarest dinosaur skeletons. According to archaeologists, the age of some of them is around 120 million years. A walk on an elegant Grand Sablon Square will surely leave great pleasure. Near the square you will also find numerous cafes, restaurants and antique shops. Car lovers will be interested to see a collection of Autoworld exhibition center. Here you will find one of the world's finest collections of antique cars. You will find here as many as 450 cars from different countries of the world.

Beautiful Cathedral of the Virgin Mary, built in the early 14th century, is an important historical landmark of the city. Its walls are home to old statues. Many interesting legends are connected with these statues and you will definitely hear them during your excursion. Church of Sacre Coeur is one of five largest religious monuments in the world. The building of the church was completed only in 1960 it lasted more than a hundred years. The number of chapels in the basilica represents the number of provinces of Belgium (all 9 provinces), which is also very symbolic. Cathedral of St. John the Baptist is also the landmark visiting which is recommended to all travellers. The construction of the church started in 1657. The church is made in Baroque style and this is one of the most remarkable religious buildings of Belgium.

Impressive tourists will be amazed by interesting sculptures located on the territory of the capital of Belgium. The famous "Manneken Pis" is not the only interesting monument in the city. By the way, in the capital of Belgium there is also a statue of "Jeanneke-Pis". Among the other notable monuments you will come across are De Vaartkapoen, the most fun-generated statue in Brussels, and Everard't Serclaes, which is striking with its mysticism. There is also the Infantry Memorial, built specifically to remind the people of their heroes. Guests who enjoy cultural recreations in nature will like Bois de la Cambre. It is a place where you can conduct a wonderful hike, as well as organize a picnic.

Hometown of Audrey Hepburn is one great attraction, where at every step there are interesting buildings. Among the most notable is the Cathédrale des StsMichel et Gudule a place that simply amazes with its magnificence and grandeur. The Cathedral was built in the beginning of the XIII century. Palais Royal, the official palace of Kings and Queens of the Belgians since the 11th century, is yet another place worthy of visiting. It is not only pleasant to look at, but also aesthetically gratifying. If the king happens to be present during the time of your visit, then you will notice an honor guard at the front of the palace. If on the other hand he is in another place, a flag flies over the palace.

One of the most interesting places in the City is Porte de Hal, a building that was used as a prison, while also serving as the city gate. Today the building houses the Museum of History and Art. If you wish to get acquainted with the life of the Belgians in the XIX century as I suspect that you do, then you definitely should not pass up the opportunity to visit a certain small hidden architectural pearl called the Maison Autrique. The peculiar oasis of appeasement can be found on the "Place des Martyrs" a historic place that keeps its secrets. The square was named after the victims of the war for the independence of Belgium (1830), who were buried right in the crypt under it. In the center you can find a monument to the heroes.

For those who wish to explore the city in another way, say, the futuristic part of it, besides the above mentioned Atomium, a visit to the Heysel Exhibition Park would be perfect. In addition to the fact that the building looks quite impressive, there are interesting types of flora inside. Those who are accustomed to seeing Brussels only as a historical city will be pleasantly surprised to visit the Belgian Comic Strip Center and discover an interesting world of comic books. Also popular is The Comic Strip Walk, a kind of walk through the "places of glory" Brussels graffiti. It seems that this is a completely different city but here it is, Brussels, combining modernity and tradition.

Cathedral of St. Michael and St. Gudula, Brussels

Facts: » The Cathedral of St. Michael and St. Gudula is one of the main attractions of Brussels, and the clearest example of Gothic architecture.

» The building of the cathedral is a symmetrical composition with two towers, within which there is a long staircase opening onto the terrace that is 64 meters high. The terrace offers a magnificent view of the city.

» The Cathedral has four doors decorated with wrought-reliefs and statues of saints. There is a huge stained glass above the main entrance.

» Stained glasses decorating the cathedral were created in the 16th century by Jan Haq and in 18-19th century by Jean-Baptiste Kaproner.

» The cathedral houses the mausoleum of the Belgian national hero Frederic de Merode.

Basilica of the Sacred Heart, Brussels

Facts: » The Catholic Basilica of the Sacred Heart is dedicated to the Sacred Heart of Jesus. It was inspired by the eponymous basilica in Paris.

» This shrine is the sixth area of the Roman Catholic Church in the world.

» The church is the large structure with two towers and a green copper dome towering 89 meters above the ground. The length of the building is almost 165 meters.

» In total the church can accommodate up to 2,000 people.

» The basilica houses a restaurant, a Catholic radio station, theater, two museums, and a place of training cavers and climbers.

Royal Palace, Brussels

Facts: » The Royal Palace is the official residence of the Belgian monarch situated in the heart of the capital.

» At present the royal family palace is used mainly as a venue for formal events.

» Every summer, the Royal Palace is traditionally open to the public. You can get inside the palace and see its galleries and chambers for free.

» Throne Hall with its grand decor, a wonderful mirror room, the ceiling of which is decorated with winged scarab beetles, and the Imperial Room with gorgeous golden flower pots, where plants of eleven colors, one for each province of Belgium, are the most notable places.

» The palace also houses the museum of Bellevue, which was once a hotel accommodating many famous people. Now that's the museum of history of Belgium.

Church of Our Blessed Lady, Brussels

Facts: » The Church of Our Blessed Lady is one of the clearest examples of temples built in the late Gothic style.

» The Church was built in the period from 1400 to 1594. It's located near Small Sablon Park that was laid in honor of the great men of the sixteenth century.

» The church building is decorated with beautiful stained glass windows; bright interior lighting is turned on in the night.

» Since its construction in 1784, the church has being serving as the burial place for noble aristocratic families.

» The church is famous for its numerous sculptures adorning the facade of the building, its grounds and interior.

Royal Palace of Laeken, Brussels

Facts:» The Royal Palace of Laeken is the residence of the Belgian royal family, where it currently resides.

» The building of the palace was built in 1781-1785 in the style of Classicism.

» The Royal Palace of Laeken is also famous for its territory boasting a magnificent park, a lake, the Royal Conservatory, a golf course and various pavilions.

» The park has two buildings unusual for Belgium style. Those are the Chinese pavilion and the Japanese tower that appeared here after Leopold II visited the World's Fair in Paris in 1900; there he saw pavilions of different countries, so he wanted to decorate his park.

» Opposite the park there is the neo-Gothic Church of Our Lady in Laeken with the crypt serving as the burial place of the royal family.

» Unfortunately, the palace itself is closed to the public, but the park, pavilions and conservatory are open for everyone.

Attractions and Nightlife

City break in Brussels. Active leisure ideas for Brussels attractions, recreation and nightlife

Fans of entertainment and fun activities will find almost endless ways of fascinating pastime in Brussels. A swimming pool and an entertainment center Oceadium is ready to accept its guests all year round. This is a great destination for the whole family. When it comes to describing "night" entertainments for adults, the choice here is also quite large. When night falls to the city, here open numerous night clubs, casinos and discos. Fans of techno music style will surely enjoy visiting Fuse nightclub, which often hosts performances of DJs of the world level. Celtica is considered the most famous place among local discotheques. Guests can have fun here every evening. Excellently selected music program, high quality sound and a big, bright dance floor these are the main secrets of success of this disco.

Sparrow Club is known far beyond the city. Here you can hear music of various directions, from energetic salsa to soul. A cozy and delightful bar is another distinct feature of this club. There are always a welcoming atmosphere and a huge selection of cocktails here. The location of Le Mirano club is old cinema building. Club Le Mirano is a constant venue of conducting various fashion shows. On weekends this place is the location of colorful theme parties. Such rich cultural program of the club has attracted even celebrities, who have chosen Le Mirano a permanent place of their rest.

Mini Europe tourist complex offers a complete and exciting holiday rest. On the territory of the complex are located a water park, medicinal thermal springs, as well as several well-equipped bungalows. All visitors are free to stay in them. May is the month when numerous music lovers arrive in Brussels. The last weekend of May is the time of the annual festival of jazz.

Besides traditional sightseeing and shopping Brussels is able to provide each tourist with a possibility to relax on the highest level. A huge number of entertainment venues, movie theaters and sporting venues will delight fans of active recreation.

If you have watched and discovered all the sightseeings, and there is nothing left to entertain you do not get upset. Brussels is capable of giving to each tourist an opportunity to have a rest at the top level. The huge number of entertainment facilities, movie theatres and sports centres will please and provide with active recreation. In Brussels, you will find various QuestRooms, where you and your family, friends will spend a really fun time with benefits. We have highlighted for you the most fun and entertaining QuestRooms in the whole Brussels. Let's discover them!

On Rue de Livourne, you will find "The Escape Hunt", which is the perfect place to forget oneself for 1 hour and spend a good time with your family, friends or colleagues. By the way, this place is awesome for team building practices. Here you will have two choices of a quest: with or without tips. But how the experience shows us, without tips to complete the quest is almost impossible. Also, here you will be to choose the level of complexity. Why do we like this place a lot? The concepts of quests are changing each 6 months, that's why you will never get bored with one theme and subject of a quest. On another street Rue de l'Etuve 69, you will find the "Escape Prod", different type of escape room. You and your company will be provided with the costumes of prisoners and you will need to find the exit from this "prison". "Escape Prod" is available for all ages, from 9 till 75 years old. Your adventure will start with short briefing done by instructors.

Those, who are looking for a bright and active recreation, Brussels offers to get an amazing experience to do the dive in the deepest pool. Nemo 33 is an indoor swimming pool facility, which holds the record as the deepest swimming pool in the world! Why do you think it is called Nemo 33? The answer is very simple, the swimming pool's depth is 33 meters! The pool is located on Rue de Stalle 333 and is easily accessible by all public transport. The temperature of the water in the pool is about 28 degrees. The entrance price is about 30 euros, which includes all the necessary equipment. The diving gear is in good condition and available in all sizes. We highly recommend you to enlarge your experience by scuba-diving into the 33-meter tube with the ladder. Besides the tube, you can dive, swim and explore the pool's so-called caves, which are painted in different themes. When you finished with diving and feel empty, high time to visit the Thai food restaurant. It is worth checking out, not only because the food is delicious, but because it is a great fun to overwatch the divers in the pool. In the bar, you will find original Belgium beer

Cuisine and Restaurant

Cuisine of Brussels for gourmets. Places for dinner best restaurants

Brussels cuisine can satisfy even most demanding gourmets and those people, who like to order something "simpler". Almost every restaurant offers its guests to try their special dishes made of seafood. Salads with clams, mussels' sauce and amazingly huge selection of first courses Belgians are the authors of most original dishes made of seafood. Gourmets will appreciate scallops, grilled shrimps with vegetables, sole and smoked eel.

Of course, we simply cannot fail to mention Brussels sprouts local chefs prepare it in all possible ways. However, these dishes are considered the prerogative of the tourists; local people prefer to order baked chicory, asparagus and parsnips as vegetable garnishes. The Belgians are also known as big fans of meat dishes. Elite restaurants of the city offer to visitors such dishes as rabbit with honey sauce, pheasant medallions, and baked berry sauce pork.

Among the traditional dishes of the local cuisine Liege salad occupies its special place. This dish is made of green beans, ham and potatoes. Sweet tooth travellers should not forget to try flavored waffles, which are served in any cafe. Typically, this dessert is offered with a widest choice of fruit sauces, fresh fruits and berries. Brussels kitchen cannot be distinguished by a large choice of complicated dishes, but it remains one of the most attractive and original cuisines in the world.

Amadeus is one of the best restaurants devoted to national cuisine. The restaurant's hall is decorated in the style of past centuries. You can find many positive feedbacks and comments about dishes from this restaurant. Original nutty bread is one of main "specialties" of this restaurant. Chefs here always try to please every customer, so you will be genuinely satisfied. Lovers of gourmet cuisine can't forget to visit the restaurant named Comme Chez Soi. This hospitable place serves lobsters and truffles, roasted lamb, and excellent wine. Continue tasting exotic dishes at La Maison du Cygne restaurant. In addition to dishes from Belgian cuisine, the menu of the restaurant contains many interesting French delicacies, and wine list will surprise even connoisseurs of this drink by presence of rare varieties of the drink.

In Brussels, travelers are welcome to try all popular dishes of the Belgian cuisine, including mussels, fragrant waffles, and excellent chocolate. If you want to try a typical breakfast of local people, head to one of smaller local restaurants and order «tomates aux crevettes». This is the name for fresh tomatoes stuffed with shrimps. As a rule, this dish is served with greens. Shrimps that live in the Northern Sea are usually quite small in size, and this makes the dish look even more elegant and attractive. Garnalen shrimps are a true local specialty that travelers can find only in selected Belgian cities. These shrimps can be cooked in a number of ways. The small shrimps can be stewed in tomato sauce or fried with cheese and fresh herbs.

Mussels are also incredibly popular in Brussels, and so local chefs cook them in dozens of different ways. Mussels stewed in white wine are considered one of the most refined and gourmet ways to cook this seafood. Mussels can taste even in a more tender way if they are stewed in cream. There is one more popular national recipe of cooking mussels in melted butter. Crispy French fries are the most typical garnish to mussels. Locals have a special term for this potato dish, frieten. It is possible to purchase roasted potatoes virtually everywhere in Brussels, and it is very affordable. Experienced travelers, however, recommend trying it in small street kiosks that are located not far from Eugeny Flagey Square. It is believed that the potatoes sold on that square taste particularly amazing.

Travelers wishing to try something truly exotic and unavailable outside Brussels can always head to one of local restaurants and order paling in't groen. This is the local name of eel stew that is served together with a peculiar green sauce. The history of this dish is very interesting. Several hundred years ago, local people were catching eels in the Scheldt River. After that, they collected various herbs that grew near the river's bank, such as mint, spinach, parsley, sorrel, and lettuce. They used all these greens to make a special sauce that remains the main secret of the ever popular dish.

Gourmets in love with meat dishes will genuinely enjoy the signature Flemish carbonade, stoverij. It is cooked in dark beer and served with a no less amazing garnish, stoemp. The latter contains mashed potatoes together with various vegetables and herbs. Tourists in Brussels also like small crunchy buns that local call "pistols". These buns can come with a variety of fillings including cheese, sausages, and ham. Small sea snails are one more popular street food that is loved by both locals and tourists.

Tradition and Nightlife

Colors of Brussels traditions, festivals, mentality and lifestyle

Despite the indifferent attitude to cooking, local people prefer simple food. They always order most familiar and simple dishes in restaurants, avoiding delicacies and culinary delights. However, if travelers order a standard portion of food, the natives will certainly ask to bring them a double one people here eat a lot, even though the food is quite simple.

Brussels natives are very sociable and friendly, you can easily discuss any topic with them. Nevertheless, it is necessary to avoid talking about the government, the royal family and inter-ethnic relations. As in any other country, there are some taboos here. The local population is very intolerant to French culture, so you should never compare the natives with the residents of France. Local people do not like it when visitors start copying their accent. Such behavior is regarded as a mockery and contempt. Brussels is ahead of many European cities in the number of various national holidays and festivals. It seems that its residents are prepared to have fun every day, and sing and dance on the squares of the city from dawn till late evening.

The beginning of July is the time of a colorful folklore Ommegang festival in Brussels. On the day of the holiday local people dress up in beautiful medieval costumes, and the squares of the city become the location of interesting theatrical and musical performances. Literally, the name of the holiday can be translated as "a procession in a circle". It was celebrated for the first time on the 14th century. Originally the holiday was dedicated to the Blessed Virgin Mary, but later it lost its religious significance. Sablon Square is the main location of various celebrations. Besides a grandiose concert here is conducted a fair of artisans, where you can purchase interesting souvenirs, as well as look at the competitions in crossbow shooting. Grand Place Square is the location of a solemn procession, which involves about a half of a thousand of people. Each of them is dressed in a unique medieval costume.

Belgian capital deservedly belongs to the largest cultural centres of Europe. The glory of the city of Brussels by the rich number of cultural events and festivals, museums with precious historic antiquities and astonishing architecture. Local people dedicate a lot of time and effort to honour their long history and the most significant historic events, that now are represented in the way of festivals and carnivals.

For example, Brussels Ommegang Medieval Festival precisely displays the procession of welcoming Charles V in 1549. Only those people, who have dressed in the costumes of the 16th century are allowed to participate in this unique procession. About 1200 participants represent the members of an imperial family and court, the representatives of magistrate and different guilds, and also soldiers and citizens. This festival takes place in July, every year. Zinneke parade in Brussels, which is celebrated each two years. Every time it has new subject and scenario. For two days, the city streets transform to the theatrical platforms, where various theatrical performances take place. The main idea of this parade is to uncover the skills and abilities for improvisation among participants.

Belgian National Day is the most important and favourite holiday of the country. It is celebrated on the July 21; on the date when the country of Belgium achieved its nationhood and became independent. Local people, as well as tourists, gather on the main square of Brussels, where they can pay the tribute to the memory. The procession starts from the military parade. Later on, it is changed to fun street celebrations, filled with music and dances, speeches from the people of art, and grandiose fireworks. This is the only day when local museums open their doors for free for tourists, that is why do your best to plan the trip on this day.

If you are the art lover, follow all the new trends and faces in the art, then it's high time to visit Brussels in September October. At this time period, the Europalia International Art Festival takes place. It is held once in two years and was firstly established in 1969. During this festival, you will enjoy and expand your knowledge with the culture and heritage of one of the world countries: art, music, photography, theatre, the art of dance, poetry and literature. The main aim of Europalia festival is to strengthen the cultural status of Brussels as the capital of Belgium, as well as the promotion of European ideals. Europalia contributes to the cultural dimension of European construction by promoting Europe's diverse cultures and encouraging their dialogue with the world's great cultures.

Accommodations

Extraordinary hotels
Extraordinary hotels best choice for your unusual city break in Brussels

Brussels Welcome Hotel
From Brussels center 0.9 km
Unique Brussels Welcome Hotel show on the map will please travellers who enjoy exploring cultures of different nations. The hotel has only 15 guestrooms, each of which has its own name the Silk Road, Tahiti, Marrakech, Belgian Congo, Bali, Kenyan Safari, Egypt, India, Tibet, and so on. The beautifully decorated rooms have items brought from the above-mentioned countries or gifted to the hotel by customers. The amazing hotel never ceases to attract and amaze guests with its diversity and exclusiveness.

Zoom Hotel
From Brussels center 1.4 km
A no less interesting hotel, Zoom Hotel show on the map draws the attention of travellers with its unusual urban design. Gray is the dominating color in the hotel. Guestrooms come with beautiful light wood decoration, and some twin rooms feature large beds with canopies. Absolutely all rooms are decorated with large colorful paintings. One can also see interesting modern artworks in public zones. A charming and secluded inner yard with a bar is another advantage of the hotel. In addition to signature drinks, the bar serves best sorts of Belgian beer.

Hotel Le Dome
From Brussels center 1.4 km
Hotel Le Dome show on the map is a popular hotel on Rogier Square, which is located in a beautiful historic building. At a glance, this hotel doesn't look much different from others. Hotel Le Dome is made in an elegant style and offers a standard choice of services. However, the famous hotel has its own secret a beautiful garden on the roof of the building. Travellers will simply fall in love with this landscape zone with greenhouses, various decorations and well-equipped relaxation areas. This is a true oasis among noisy streets of the city.

Hotel BLOOM
From Brussels center 1.7 km
Often recognized as a landmark in Brussels, Hotel BLOOM show on the map is a large design hotel with more than 300 comfortable guestrooms. All guestrooms are made in different styles with white as the dominating color and interesting artistic patterns on the walls. The hotel's restaurant, Smoods, is another advantage of this magnificent place. Besides tables, the spacious hall of the restaurant has become the last resort to a retro Volkswagen minibus. By the way, one table is installed inside the bus. A dinner in such an unusual setting promises to be mesmerizing.

Radisson RED Hotel Brussels
From Brussels center 1.7 km
Radisson RED Hotel Brussels show on the map can hardly be called an ordinary hotel. It is distinguished by unusual designer approach and

style. Best and most talented teams of local designers participated in the development of the hotel's look. From the moment of its opening, the hotel has regularly hosted various interesting exhibitions, music concerts and other events that will surely attract fans of modern art. The ultra-modern hotel is distinguished by high-class technical equipment. Guests are encouraged to use RED App that enables sharing of music and photographs with other guests of the hotel.

9Hotel Central
From Brussels center 0.7 km
Travellers, who enjoy staying in an unusual setting, will like boutique hotel 9Hotel Central show on the map. It is located in a fully restored townhouse and has more than 40 rooms designed in original style. All guestrooms feature retro brick walls, stylish modern furniture and designer vintage accessories. Handmade wooden furniture, old statues and paintings, interesting works of local artisans and branded accessories this hotel looks more like an interesting art gallery or an art museum.

Stylish design-hotels
Stylish weekend in Brussels collection of top unique boutique hotels
Tenbosh House
From Brussels center 2.7 km
Exclusive mini hotel Tenbosh House show on the map is a relatively new hotel in Brussels. It was decided to make the hotel in

Scandinavian style that combines aesthetics and functionality. Designers carefully selected furniture made in the middle of the previous century, so it would leave plenty of free space and help to create calm and serene atmosphere. The light colored lobby of the hotel is decorated with retro photographs. The owner of the hotel is a big fan of modern art, so she regularly invites designers and artists to communicate with them and lets them change the design of her hotel.

Pantone Hotel
From Brussels center 1.3 km
One more artistic hotel, Pantone Hotel show on the map is the first hotel made in accordance with color schemes developed by the American company Pantone in the middle of the XX century. The designer team decided to make every floor on the basis of one of the seven rainbow colors. Exclusive guestrooms, which are decorated with designer furniture and unique installations of photographer Victor Levi, look like true pieces of art. This hotel will be liked by travellers who are keen on art and quality design.

Bloom Hotel
From Brussels center 1.7 km
When it was time to renovate the rooms, Bloom Hotel show on the map decided to make something creative. They invited 300 young artists aged 15 and below, who were asked to decorate the rooms with flower patterns. The décor is made in two color schemes a light and a dark one. In case some travellers are not fond of such art, 18

rooms at the hotel are left without any drawings. Pamper yourself with a stylish stay at Bloom hotel, and you will surely have many pleasant memories.

The design of Exclusive The White Hotel was developed by as many as 70 popular Belgian designers. Large crispy white rooms with light curtains feature either an exclusive decoration or an installation created specifically for that room. Everything at this hotel is made around design, so art connoisseurs would find their stay at Exclusive The White Hotel very pleasing.

Aloft Brussels Schuman
From Brussels center 2.1 km
Aloft Brussels Schuman show on the map was the first hotel in Europe operating under the Aloft brand. This is a modern hotel targeted at young travellers, so it features catchy design and many socializing options. Quite spacious rooms with very high ceilings of up to three meters are made in the open space manner, and furniture is used to separate one functional zone from another. Aloft promises luxurious style at a reasonable price, so this hotel will be a wonderful choice for all travellers.

Royal Windsor Hotel Grand Place
From Brussels center 0.3 km
Exclusive design in royal style has become one of the main peculiarities and advantages of posh Royal Windsor Hotel Grand Place show on the map. Its guestrooms feature an eye-catching design with

rare materials used premium sorts of wood and elegant antique furniture. Twin rooms feature large bedrooms with canopies, and some guestrooms have several functional zones separated by draping. All rooms are decorated with branded textiles, genuine artworks and vintage accessories. Public zone of the hotel come with authentic antique furniture.

Hotels with history

Preserved history of Brussels: long-standing and historical hotels

Metropole Hotel

From Brussels center 0.9 km

Metropole Hotel show on the map is the only historic hotel that has survived since 1895 and has façade and ground floor protected as landmarks. The magnificent, luxurious and posh hotel has a big lobby made in the Empire style. Inside, travellers will find beautifully decorated ceiling, marble walls, sparkling crystal chandeliers and numerous comfortable sofas. The grand hall has marble ladders that lead to rooms that differ in size, style and décor. Breakfasts are served in the hall that has same planning and design as the Indian temple of Akshardham. During its long history, the hotel has welcomed many famous people, including composer Arthur Rubinstein, French actor Philippe Noiret, tennis player Justine Henin, physicist David Gross, French writer Pierre Arditi, and many more. The luxurious design of the hotel was used for filming purposes of such movies as Les anges gardiens (Guardian Angles) and Le Sang des autres (The Blood of Others).

Hotel Manos Stephanie
From Brussels center 1.4 km

Travellers, who are fond of staying at historic hotels in Brussels, are recommended to pay attention to Hotel Manos Stephanie show on the map, which is located right in the heart of the city, not far from Avenue Louise. This magnificent hotel will bring its guests to the elegant period of Louis XVI. The hotel simply strikes visitors with its outstanding design and genuine antiquities. Behind the entrance doors, guests will find a spacious hall with marble columns and crystal chandeliers. Guests of the hotel will be delighted with spacious rooms with high ceilings, which are decorated with vintage furniture and posh textiles.

Hotel Aspria Royal La Rasante
From Brussels center 5.7 km

If a countryside vacation sounds very appealing to you, take a look at Hotel Aspria Royal La Rasante show on the map which is located in an old farmer's mansion. The building was reconstructed, but much of the original design and decorations have been kept. There are only 19 rooms at this hotel, and all of them feature massive wooden furniture and natural textiles. Some rooms still feature original beam joint and mansard ceiling. Among advantages of the hotel, it's simply impossible to fail to mention a wonderful spa and a lush garden.

Hotel Mozart

Brussels center 0.3 km

The center of the historic part of Brussels is the location of another magnificent hotel, Hotel Mozart show on the map. This hotel is also located in a beautiful historic building. Hotel Mozart differs from other historic hotels. It is made in posh Middle Eastern style and looks more like a sultan's palace rather than a hotel. Its walls and ceiling are decorated with skillful paintings and colorful ceramic tiles. Priceless antique furniture, nearly all pieces of which are handmade, makes the hotel look like a fairy-tale place. Bright lamps in oriental style, giant chandeliers, ancient paintings in carved frames and elements with gilding Hotel Mozart will simply strike its visitors with grandeur.

Hotel Noga

From Brussels center 1.1 km

A charming house not far from the old fishing market of St. Catherine has become home for Hotel Noga show on the map. A team of talented designers worked hard to create a warm and pleasant atmosphere of the middle of the 20th century. Walls in rooms are covered with cute vintage wallpapers and feature colorful textiles carefully selected in accordance with trends of the past. Many rooms and public zones are decorated with interesting vintage items beautiful furniture, paintings, ship models, hand-painted vases and lamps, antique carpets and other interesting accessories that will certainly draw the attention of history fans.

Luxury accommodation

Top places to stay in Brussels most luxury and fashionable hotels

Steigenberger Grandhotel

From Brussels center 1.3 km

The opening of Steigenberger Grandhotel show on the map under a new brand took place in the beginning of 2013. The magnificent building of the 19th century simply strikes with its spacious elegant hall with marble floor and shiny candelabrums. The exclusive grand hotel features spacious rooms designed in accordance with individual projects in a classic and elegant style. Guests of Steigenberger Grandhotel are always welcome at Aspira Avenue Louise wellness centre, a bar and a terrace with charming views of the city. There are also exhibition halls at the hotel that can be visited by guests.

Hotel Amigo Brussels

From Brussels center 0.3 km

After a thorough restoration, Hotel Amigo Brussels show on the map has returned its title of the best hotel in Brussels. The designer decoration of interiors is made in red or dark-green colors. Not only exceptional condition of rooms, but also state-of-art technical functionality will leave many pleasant memories about your stay at this amazing hotel.

The owner of Hotel Manos Premier Constantin Poulgouras offers the hospitality of the highest class. Upon entering the hotel, you will find yourself in the world of uniqueness and luxury. Genuine antique furniture and artworks that date back to Louis XV period were selected by best collectors. Crystal chandeliers, historic items, baroque showcases and exceptionally luxurious rooms are worth a king. However, despite such luxury, the hotel is very charming and even home-like. A 2,000 sq. meters large private garden with lush greenery, singing birds and gurgling water is another advantage of Hotel Manos Premier Constantin Poulgouras as it is really hard to find a place like this in a modern capital. Manos Premier is a hotel that emphasizes charm and atmosphere of Brussels.

Le Plaza
From Brussels center 1.3 km
The design of hotel Le Plaza show on the map was inspired by the famous Parisian hotel George V. Inner décor of the hotel is no less refine and elegant than its French paragon. Antique furniture, crystal chandeliers, marble floors and expensive carpets create the elegant style of the '30s of the previous century. There are some antique areas at the hotel, such as the theater hall with unique décor in the Mauritian style. Sticking to traditions of aristocratic luxury, the hotel, nevertheless, harmoniously combines them with modern comfort.

Stanhope Hotel
From Brussels center 1.2 km
Stanhope Hotel show on the map was the first five-star hotel in Belgium. The design of the magnificent hotel is reminiscent of a prestigious residence in the classic English style. Elegant premium

furniture, exclusive flower pattern textiles, amazing painting and Chinese white and blue vases make the hotel look very solid and posh. The hotel also features a picturesque garden with a fountain, and charming bar and restaurant designed like a royal banquet hall and decorated with busts of members of royal families. One can always hear classic music in the hall of the hotel.

Hotel Sofitel Brussels Europe
From Brussels center 2.2 km
Luxury travellers usually praise Hotel Sofitel Brussels Europe show on the map that features posh modern design rooms. Many rooms come with large floor to ceiling windows, and couples will like twin rooms with special glass wall bathrooms. One of the most famous restaurants in the city, BE Café Marché Jourdan, is also located at the hotel. Windows of the restaurant offer breath-taking views of Brussels, and during warm months guests are welcome to relax on a special terrace on the roof of the building.

Romantic hotels

Brussels for couples in love best hotels for intimate escape, wedding or honeymoon
Odette en Ville
From Brussels center 2.1 km
It's hard not to get affected by the charm of the small boutique hotel of Odette en Ville show on the map. Its unique style can be seen everywhere from the trendy hall to guestrooms. The hotel will be

particularly liked by travellers who wish to have a secluded vacation. Gas powered fireplaces and large Jacuzzi baths in rooms only help to enjoy a relaxing and peaceful stay at the hotel. In the evening, it's time to head to the hotel's bar to enjoy a wonderful dinner in a romantic setting with lots of candles.

B&B Maison d Hôtes Osiam
From Brussels center 0.6 km
B&B Maison d Hôtes Osiam show on the map is a paradise like place for romantic travellers and couples. The hotel has a private Japanese style garden that is perfect for a romantic and private walk. Travellers are also welcome to attend both indoor and outdoor swimming pools of the hotel or enjoy relaxing treatments at the hotel's spa. Rooms are very comfortable and feature a fridge, a microwave oven, a Senseo coffee machine, delicious chocolate and waffles. B&B Maison d Hôtes Osiam is located among romantic streets, so it's a great destination for travellers who want to explore the historic part of Brussels and its architectural landmarks.

Be Manos
From Brussels center 0.9 km
Be Manos show on the map is an ideal place for travellers who want to spend an unforgettable vacation in Brussels. A team of professional European designers thoroughly worked over every slightest detail in order to make the hotel one of the trendiest places in the city. Guests of Be Manos will be glad to spend their free time in the luxurious spa

center with Russian bath and recreation rooms. Romantic dinners at premium Be Lella restaurant will make your stay at the hotel even more pleasant and will leave many pleasant memories.

Monty Small Design Hotel
From Brussels center 3.9 km
Miniature and inexpensive Monty Small Design Hotel show on the map is located in a very beautiful old house. This hotel will draw the attention of travellers who are fond of non-standard designer ideas and designer approach. Red color, which dominates in the hotel's design, makes travellers more active, maintaining the atmosphere of love and passion. The hotel is proud of its informal style of service. There is no restaurant at the hotel, so guests are invited to have breakfast and dinner at one big table installed in the lounge zone. During their stay at the hotel, travellers are welcome to use bicycles to explore the city or leisurely relax in the garden or on the terrace, away from city noise and stress.

Hotel Barsey by Warwick
From Brussels center 2.9 km
Luxurious Hotel Barsey by Warwick show on the map is a great place for couples who seek a hotel for a romantic vacation. Mostly made in bright and bold colors, the hotel offers elegant rooms for couples. These rooms come with luxurious designer furniture and premium textiles. In some rooms, a part of the wall, which separates the bathroom from the rest of the room, is replaced with a glass divider.

Guests can also choose a room with a private furnished balcony, and during warm months travellers are always welcome to relax in the charming inner yard with an old fountain.

The Dominican
From Brussels center 0.7 km
Only a short walk separates Grand Place from boutique hotel The Dominican show on the map that also attracts guests with its romantic and refined design. The rooms mostly feature trendy contemporary look and are decorated with luxurious paintings in the Renaissance style. The hotel has simply everything needed for a comfortable stay a stylish lounge with a rich choice of treats and a bar with a wide choice of exotic cocktails. Besides that, travellers are always welcome at the spa with sauna and massage rooms.

Shopping in Brugge

Shopping in Brussels authentic goods, best outlets, malls and boutiques
In Brussels, there are more than a hundred shopping streets with interesting shops on each of them. Among the most popular is Neuve Street. It is here, that the wealthiest travellers go shopping. Here, are some exclusive designer boutiques, where they sell readymade and custom-made designer clothes. For those, who are not accustomed to spending huge sums on clothes, there are several perfect stores on

this street. Among the latter, trading pavilions Mexx, Benetton, H&M, Woman's Secret Zara, Diesel and New Look are worth mentioning.

To buy elite clothes and accessories, you should go to Louise Avenue. Here, are boutiques of Louis Vuitton, Tommy Hilfiger, Chanel, Hermes, Gucci, Christian Dior and Cartier world famous brands. The main customers of local shops are tourists, so it's not surprising that prices here are slightly over the top. But buyers can always expect to high quality clothes, perfumes and jewelry.

Among the most attractive and unusual shopping complexes of the city is the Royal Galleries of St. Hubert. This shopping arcade occupies a complex of beautiful historical buildings. A huge area of the complex is covered by a single glass roof. This shopping center is the largest in the city. Besides the stores, there are several restaurants and cafes, confectioneries, as well as a fascinating musical theater. The variety of goods presented in the shopping center is also striking. It sells clothes and footwear of world famous brands, cosmetics and perfumery, jewelry and household goods and very cute souvenirs in national style.

Travellers who want to bring from their trip stylish designer things, should go to Rue Antoine-Dansaer. On this street boutiques of famous Belgian designers, in which buyers are offered trendy things for every taste, are concentrated. An important attractive feature of these designer stores are affordable prices. They are much lower than in many popular designer stores in Europe. Designer clothes presented in this district are very popular with world celebrities. Royal families order tailoring here, for example.

In Brussels, run several wonderful antique markets, a walk through them will also give you a lot of impressions. In the city you will also find a world famous Place du Grand Sablon market, which is the largest antique market, not only in Belgium, but also in Europe. A variety of antiquities that can be seen here is amazing. Ancient candlesticks, pieces of furniture, great paintings and statuettes, vintage jewelry and accessories for house are just a part of the stuff presented here. Among such a huge choice of antiques, experienced collectors find many rare items.

A walk through the largest in the city Chatelain food market, which is located on the square with the same name, near the South Station, will turn out to be a particular event. This market sells the freshest products from all regions of the country. Lovers of eco-friendly dairy and meat products will especially love it here. In several tents popular street food and sweets are sold. This market is a popular local and tourist walking destination. In Brussels, walking along historical shopping streets and popular markets can turn into an exciting excursion.

Tourist Tips

Preparing your trip to Brussels: advices & hints things to do and to obey

1. Weather is rather rainy in Brussels, so tourists, who plan to make long walks, are recommended to take a raincoat or an umbrella with them.

2. Summer is considered the best time to travel to Brussels. The temperature here rarely exceeds +18°C, and rains are quite rare during this period, so nothing will break your recreation program.

3. If elegant clothing and perfumes are your aim, move your feet to shopping centers located on Waterloo and Louise Streets. These parts of the city are known as the location of elite boutiques and jewelry stores.

4. Products made of crystal, chocolate and lace will become best souvenirs. Connoisseurs of expensive alcoholic beverages may purchase local gin as a souvenir.

5. Comics are considered one of the main and unique attractions of the city. A whole museum Comic Strip is devoted to heroes of colorful magazines. You will see a large toy store near the museum. This is the place where the locals recommend going for gifts for children.

6. Currency can be exchanged at banks or special exchange offices. As a rule, banks are closed during the day for lunch. Saturday and Sunday

are also days off. Currency exchange offices are more likely to work on weekends and during lunch breaks.

7. Tourists are recommended to be vigilant in crowded places. Despite the fact that Brussels is one of the safest cities of the country, there may be pickpockets in public transport and at markets. Do not leave belongings unattended at restaurants and cafes. We also do not recommend taking large amounts of money with you unless it's necessary.

8. Remote areas of the city are best to be visited with a guide, but the central area is very quiet and crowded. Even late at night you can meet here numerous tourists and locals, who make their evening walk

The End

Printed in the USA
CPSIA information can be obtained
at www.ICGtesting.com
LVHW092150230823
756118LV00036B/555